SCENES FROM THE PAST

WIGAN
TO
PRESTON

THE NORTH UNION LINE
REMEMBERED

A Glasgow (Central) to London (Euston) express passing through Leyland station on 23rd May 1959 headed by Stanier Princess Coronation Class '8P' 4-6-2 No **46243** *City of Lancaster*. Built in 1940, the Pacific was allocated to Camden (1B) at the end of May, and moved to Liverpool Edge Hill (8A) during week ending 5th June 1948, a further move to Crewe North (5A) in December the same year, saw 46243 spend the next ten years at the Crewe depot. Withdrawn from Edge Hill during week ending 12th September 1964, to where it had returned on the 11th March 1961, *City of Lancaster* was subsequently photographed in unfamiliar surroundings at Central Wagon Co, Ince, Wigan, on 29th May 1965, awaiting its turn for the cutting torch - see page 20. It was reported as having been scrapped by September.

Ray Farrell

RAY FARRELL

PRINTED BY AMADEUS PRESS
    CLECKHEATON, WEST YORKSHIRE.

PUBLISHED BY
FOXLINE PUBLICATIONS LIMITED
    PO BOX 84, BREDBURY. SK6 3YD

This is the signalman's view looking south from Wigan No 2 box on 28th May 1960. Stanier Jubilee class '6P5F' 4-6-0 No **45625** *Sarawak* of Crewe North (5A) heads a relief for Carlisle on the Down Main line after departure from North Western station's platform 3. To the right of the rear of the train is the northern bay 5, with platforms 4 and 5, both occupied, further to the right. Another Jubilee, No **45595** *Southern Rhodesia* awaits the route north with a parcels train from platform 4, whilst an unidentified Stanier Class '5' 4-6-0 stands at platform 5. *Sarawak* was to move to Carnforth (24L/10A) during May 1962 from where it was withdrawn in September 1963.   *Ray Farrell*

WIGAN TO PRESTON
THE 'NORTH UNION' LINE REMEMBERED

The 20mph speed restriction placed on all main lines through Preston station between signal boxes No 5 and No 1 will have been a frustration to the crew of Princess Coronation Class 4-6-2 No **46238** *City of Carlisle* at the head of the Up 'Royal Scot' (dep Glasgow 10am). Seen here passing through the village of Euxton between Euxton Junction and Balshaw Lane on 11th April 1959, the 'Duchess', having climbed continuously for the last five miles or so, takes advantage of a reverse change in gradient of just over a mile to tackle a shorter ascent to Coppull Hall Sidings, highest point between Preston and Wigan. The crew will be content with a speed of approximately 60 to 65 mph at this point. Built in September 1939, the Pacific spent its first month at Crewe North (5A) and was then to alternate between Camden (1B) and Upperby (12B) on four occasions. It was withdrawn from Upperby during September 1964 having spent its last twelve years based at the Carlisle depot.
Ray Farrell

INTRODUCTION

The route connecting London Euston and Glasgow Central covers a distance of 401¼ miles and under the auspices of initially the London Midland and Scottish Railway and subsequently British Railways, provided a continuous rail link between the two cities. Although operated by those two concerns as a single entity, the development of the route embraced a wide range of individual railway companies, which through a series of mergers and take overs eventually became known as the West Coast Main Line. The complexity of the development is well illustrated in the 141-mile section from Crewe to Carlisle which numbered no less than eight constituent companies within its embrace.

Lancaster & Carlisle.
Lancaster & Preston Junction.
North Union.
Wigan Branch
Liverpool & Manchester.
Warrington & Newton.
Grand Junction.
London & North Western.

This book is a pictorial record covering the last 10 years of British Railways steam (1958 – 1968) and early main line diesel workings of one such section – the Wigan Springs Branch to Preston section of the former North Union Railway (NU) – which formed a vital link in the overall scheme.

Even that apparently simple undertaking, covering just 22½ miles of route from Parkside, on the Liverpool & Manchester Railway to Preston, resulted from the amalgamation in May 1834 of the Wigan Branch Railway and the then still to be built Preston & Wigan Railway to form the North Union Railway, railway's first recorded merger.

The Wigan Branch Railway was incorporated on 29th May 1830, sponsored by a group of influential merchants in the Wigan area seeking a cheaper alternative than the canal system of transportation, and anxious not only to develop their own trading, but aware of the potential for passenger traffic in the future. Authorized share capital of the Wigan Branch was £70,000 with an additional borrowing power of £17,500. All capital had to be fully subscribed before construction of the line could begin.

Charles Blacker Vignoles was appointed as engineer to the Wigan Branch in June 1830 at an annual salary of £500. The first activity of the railway company was to erect a grandstand near Parkside on the Liverpool & Manchester Railway for the directors to witness the official opening of that route on 15th September 1830, a ceremony marred by tragedy.

Travelling in the first of eight trains to leave Liverpool for Manchester, hauled by locomotive *Northumbrian* and driven by George Stephenson, was the then Prime Minister, The Duke of Wellington. During a stop at Parkside for water, William Huskisson M.P. alighted from the train to talk to the Prime Minister and was struck by *Rocket* hauling the third of the day's specials on the adjoining line and driven by Joseph Locke, sustaining fatal injuries.

The 6.9 mile line from Wigan to Parkside, where the Wigan Branch connected with the Liverpool & Manchester Railway at the east facing curve in the Manchester direction, was officially opened on 3rd September 1832, some two years and two months after Vignoles appointment. Whilst the Act of Incorporation provided for a west facing curve at Parkside and also a 2.6 mile branch south of Wigan, to be known as the Springs Branch, neither were built by the Wigan Branch due to lack of finance.

Less than one year after the Wigan Branch Act was passed, an Act incorporating the Preston & Wigan Railway was approved on 22nd April 1831. With a share capital of £250,000 and borrowing powers of £83,000 to construct the 15½ mile route linking the two towns, construction could not begin until the capital was fully subscribed. This was not achieved.

By mid-1833, work on the line not having commenced, the directors considered abandoning the project, but instead approached the directors of the Wigan Branch following a meeting on 8th August of that year, with a view to consolidating the two companies and forming the North Union Railway.

The Wigan Branch directors, some of whom were also directors of the Preston & Wigan, and who themselves had financial problems of their own, readily agreed to the merger at a meeting held on 28th August 1833.

An Act consolidating the two companies by incorporating the North Union Railway was passed on 22nd May 1834, the authorised capital not to exceed that of the two constituents i.e., £320,000; with borrowing powers raised to £160,000. Sir Thomas Dalrymple Hesketh, Bart; was elected as the first chairman, a position he had held with the Preston & Wigan.

Construction of the Preston to Wigan line was not without it's difficulties. The first construction contracts were not placed until January 1835. Thereafter the combination of Chief Engineer Vignoles, appointed in June 1834, erratic behaviour and the poor performance of some contractors combined to extend the building of the line to over 3½ years, the public opening of the 22½ mile route from Parkside to Preston being on 31st October 1838, at the same time as the Springs Branch was opened.

Stanier 'Mogul' Class '6P5F' 2-6-0 No **42955** heads a 10 coach passenger train, comprised mainly of Eastern Region stock, south on 28th May 1960, having left North Western station. There is a possibility that this train was the 12.58pm ex-Preston to Crewe with through carriage facilities between Blackpool and Birmingham. Built in December 1933 and allocated new to Kentish Town (14B), the locomotive had by this time moved to Crewe South (5B) and was finally withdrawn whilst at Heaton Mersey (9F) during April 1966.

Ray Farrell

Stanier 'Jubilee' Class '6P5F' 4-6-0 No **45726** *Vindictive* heads south past Wigan Springs Branch No 1 Signal Box with 1G20, the 12.15 pm Blackpool North – Birmingham New Street on 24th June 1961. Springs Branch No 1 Box, an 80 lever LNW frame was situated between the Down Slow line and the Down St. Helens line. The Motive Power Depot (8F) was located on the east side of the main line, immediately behind the train, which coincidentally is passing over the junction with the Manchester line (ET&W), noted by the duplicity of rails on both of the fast lines. The Jubilee, built in October 1936 was allocated new to Low Moor (56F), and finally withdrawn from Warrington Dallam (8B) during March 1965.　　*Ray Farrell*

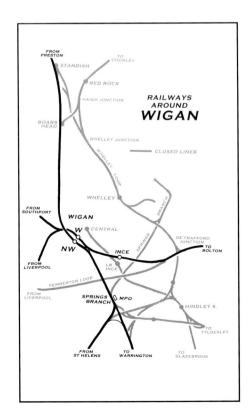

Situated less than 1 1/2 miles south of Wigan North Western Station, Springs Branch encompassed a wide variety of railway activity which in the last 10 years of British Railways steam operation witnessed a regular parade of steam hauled freight and passenger workings - interspersed in the later years with an increasing number of diesel locomotives and multiple units - traversing the numerous routes passing through and around the area.

The main line, which was quadrupled as early as 1895, ran southwards from Wigan paralleled by the East Goods lines as far as Bamfurlong, where after passing under the former Lancashire Union line at Fir Tree House Junction, the goods lines accessed the sorting sidings via a burrowing junction under the continuing main line, emerging on the western side of the Down Slow main line.

From the extensive sorting sidings situated on the west of the main line at Bamfurlong, traffic went out via the Whelley Loop to Coppull or Chorley, or on to the former Lancashire & Yorkshire route at De Trafford Junction where, having travelled with the banker on the front, they reversed and the rear engine then became the train engine.

With the exception of the former L&NWR Manchester line all routes could be accessed from the sidings. If that route was required, trains simply reversed to Ince Moss Junction and then travelled eastwards via Tyldesley to Manchester.

Dominating the railway scene in the area was the former L&NWR Motive Power Depot situated at Springs Branch on the east side of the running lines. Designated 10A from January 1935 during LMS days, the shed was re-classified 8F by BR with effect from 21st April 1958, a code it was to retain, being closed to steam from 4th December 1967, but surviving still as a diesel storage/repair depot.

Springs Branch was basically a freight shed with an allocation numbering 57 locomotives in September 1950, 67 in March 1959 and 58 in April 1965.

In 1952 following the closure of nearby Lower Ince Shed, a number of class 'J10' 0-6-0's were acquired, and with the demise of Wigan L & Y depot in 1964 and subsequent transfer of its occupants, Springs Branch had at times nearly 100 locomotives on shed.

Just south of the locomotive depot the former L&NWR 'Eccles, Tyldesley & Wigan' route to Manchester turned eastwardly a short distance beyond Springs Branch No 1 signal box. It opened on 1st September 1864. At this point, the six lines of the 'North Union' and four of the ET&W were crossed by Taylors Lane, carried on two bridges across the railway; No. 30, over the NU, had spans of 47'-10"(over slow and fast lines) and 25'-3", the latter crossing the East Goods lines; No. 82 (on the ET&W) with a single span of 48'-3" over four lines, the Up and Down Main and Up and Down Goods, this quadrupled section continuing as far as Platt Bridge Junction on the Manchester route, part of which had closed (as far as Tyldesley) to passenger traffic on 2nd November 1964.

Barely 100 yards south of Taylors Lane, bridge 29, with almost identical spans of 47'-8" and 25'-10" carried the Whelley Loop and connections from the Manchester direction over the North Union towards Ince Moss Junction and St. Helens, and also provided access to the Eccles & Tyldesley line and to the northbound main line at Standish Junction via the Whelley Loop. Specials from the East Midlands and east of the Pennines to Blackpool could travel via either Glazebrook or Tyldesley before heading through Hindley & Platt Bridge Station to join the down Whelley Loop and thence on to the NU at Standish.

The Ince Moss Junction – Whelley line opened on 1st November 1869 with the link to the main line at Standish completed on 5th June 1882. Passenger services from Wigan North Western via Chorley to Blackburn were withdrawn on 4th January 1960, the Whelley Loop surviving until 2nd October 1972.

On the same day that Ince Moss to Whelley was opened, the route linking Wigan North Western to St. Helens via Bryn also opened, bearing west immediately north of Springs Branch No. 1 box. The box, with an 80-lever L&NWR frame and situated between the Down Slow (main line) and the Down St. Helens line, was closed on 1st October 1972, concurrently with the inuaguration of the Weaver Junction to Glasgow electrification.

Springs Branch No. 2 signal box, a 90-lever LMS frame and box, was situated 417 yards north of No. 1 box between the Up Fast (main line) and the Down East Goods Line.

South of No. 2 box, the Springs Branch goods line, opened by the North Union on 31st October 1838, headed off the main line in a north easterly direction, providing access to the numerous coal mines and steelworks which had developed in the Ince and surrounding areas. The line also provided access to the Central Wagon Company depot situated about 1 mile from the junction with the main line.

Previously occupied by the Chorley Wagon Company, the site at Ince had been taken over in 1911 by the Central Wagon Company, initially to repair and/or scrap wagons from the vast number utilized in the local industries. By the late 1950's the company had moved into the locomotive scrapping business, nearly 300 locomotives meeting their demise at Ince by the time steam was finally withdrawn from British Railways in August 1968.

A most notable victim was Stanier Pacific No 46243 *City of Lancaster* which had the distinction of hauling the last steam powered 'CALEDONIAN' and was cut up during 1965. The stub of the branch behind Springs Branch depot remained in use for the shunting/storage of coal (MGR) wagons latterly serving Bickershaw Colliery until the demise of Lancashire coal fields.

The subsidence riven and spoil tip dominated landscape around Wigan is now but a memory but here briefly revived as this view of Stanier Class '5' 4-6-0 No **45293** shows it climbing the 1 in 86 gradient from Ince Moss Junction towards Fir Tree House Junction with a Ford car train from Halewood (Ford Sidings) to Bathgate on 29th May 1965. The train would travel via the undulating Whelley Loop, thus avoiding Wigan North Western before joining the main line at Standish Junction. At Fir Tree House Junction, the diverging route accessed the ET&W to Platt Bridge Junction via an adverse 1 in 77 grade. The rear of the train is passing Ince Moss Junction signal box, where the St Helens line (to Wigan), diverges to descend a modest 1 in 258 before joining the North Union at Springs Branch No 1 signal box. Introduced to traffic at Shrewsbury (84G) on 23rd December 1936, the Class '5' was at this time based at Carlisle Kingmoor (12A) and was withdrawn from there before the end of August 1965. *Ray Farrell*

(Above) Second in the sequence of three photographs which show 45293 heading its train of Ford cars/vans over the intersection bridge (over the Euston-Glasgow line) at Fir Tree House Junction. The engine would have no respite until passing the signal box and water tank. Retimed some months earlier with an amended reporting number (4S47), the train had the option of additional motive power (Class 4) if necessary. The one hour and two minutes allowed to reach Fir Tree House appears optimistic for the lengthy train but a 'round the houses' journey through Widnes and St Helens didn't do men or machine any favours. An optional ten minutes water stop at Ince Moss Junction was occasionally avoided to counter the impending climb ahead. *Ray Farrell*

(Right) An unidentified English Electric type '4' heads a Scottish bound express on the Down Fast on 29th May 1965 whilst Stanier Class Five No **45293** passes overhead on the former

Lancashire Union line in the third and final sequence of views showing it at the head of the Ford car train which will take the Whelley Loop past De Trafford Junction, and in doing so avoid Wigan North Western Station before rejoining the main line at Standish Junction (arr 2.40pm). Throughout the pages of this book, reporting numbers and train identification codes will appear occasionally and such is the complexity of it that without a specific Working Timetable, Supplement to the WTT or Weekly Notice, it becomes difficult to identify a particular working. The first panel of the four-character indicator panel on the diesel loco identifies a Class A train (the number 1) - express passenger in this case. The second position, letter 'S', indicates the Destination District (Scotland). The third and fourth positions are for individual train numbers which vary for different destinations, although the certainty in this instance is that it is a Scottish town or city. Visible immediately to the left of the Class '5' is the CWS Glass Works at Platt Bridge. *RayFarrell*

'Britannia' Class '7P6F' 4-6-2 No **70053** *Moray Firth* heads a northbound freight on the Down Fast line past the adjacent Fir Tree House Junction where the former Lancashire Union line crossed the Euston to Glasgow (West Coast Main Line) between Springs Branch and Bamfurlong Sidings. The lines in the foreground, the Up and Down East goods, ran parallel for some distance before a short rapid descent gave access to and from Bamfurlong Sidings via a burrowing junction under both fast and slow lines. The Britannia in keeping with its name began life at Polmadie (66A) and was withdrawn from Carlisle (Kingmoor - 12A) during April 1967. *Ray Farrell*

View southwards at Springs Branch on 4th June 1966. Passing on the Up Fast at 6.55pm is the Locomotive Club of Great Britain (L.C.G.B). 'Fellsman' Rail Tour double headed by a pair of Stanier Jubilee Class '6P5F' 4-6-0's No **45593** *Kolhapur* and double chimneyed No **45596** *Bahamas*. Curving away to the right (west) in front of Springs Branch No.1 box is the former Lancashire Union (LUR) route to Liverpool via Ince Moss Junction and St Helens. No.1.box, an 80 lever LNWR frame, which was located between the Down Slow and the St.Helens Down line, was closed on 1st October 1972. As suggested by the proximity of their numbers, the 'Jubilees' were built within two weeks of each other and both allocated to Crewe North (5A), *Kolhapur* on New Years Eve 1934, and *Bahamas* on 12 January 1935. Both locomotives are now preserved. The rail tour had commenced at London Euston the same morning, starting with electric haulage to Liverpool Lime Street in the hands of English Electric (Vulcan Foundry) built Bo-Bo Class AL6 No **E3169** (later 86 239 and named L S Lowry in November 1980). The next stage from Lime Street was via St Helens Shaw Street and Wigan (NW) to Carnforth, 'Britannia' Class No 70004 *William Shakespeare* in charge. 'Black Five' No 44767 came on at Carnforth, assisting 70004 over Shap to Carlisle and then Quintinshill (site of the rail disaster of 22nd May 1915). Utilising the loops at Quintinshill to provide a 'terminus' for the outward journey, the two Jubilees seen above took over the tour, returning to Crewe via Ais Gill, Hellifield, Blackburn and Wigan and the location of this photograph. According to *The Railtour Files*, due to the overhead wires having been brought down on the Trent Valley line, D302 and E3174 took the special from Crewe and Stafford via Bescot and Coventry to Rugby, where the diesel came off and the remainder of the tour to Euston was completed by E3174. *Ray Farrell*

Stanier Class '5' 4-6-0 No **45109**, at this time a Springs Branch (8F) locomotive, brings a train from Manchester over the final yards of the Eccles, Tyldesley and Wigan route to join the Down Main Euston to Glasgow line at Springs Branch (No 1) on 24th June 1961. The junction, enabling the two L&NWR routes to come together, was opened in September 1864, the resultant structures carrying Taylors Lane spanning all ten lines of the final track layout of the two routes. Not the most direct route between Manchester and Wigan, it is perhaps not surprising the service was withdrawn, when, on 2nd November 1964, along with stations on the CLC Wigan Central to Glazebrook section, the line lost its local passenger services. South Lancashire was well blessed with public transport and although the town of Tyldesley and nearby Leigh retained a service until 1969, they had more than most to lose and to this day are at the centre one of the largest conurbations in the country without a rail connection to the national network. No 45109, built in May 1935 and allocated to Crewe North (5A), survived until April 1967 when it was withdrawn from Warrington Dallam (8B).   *Ray Farrell*

Stanier Jubilee Class '6P5F' 4-6-0 No **45593** *Kolhapur* heads north with The South and West Railway Railway Society's 'Granite City' rail tour on 3rd September 1966. This ambitious event, over the weekend of 3rd/4th September, left Euston for Crewe at 09.00 hauled by British Rail/English Electric Bo-Bo Class AL6 **E3136** (later **86 044** and revised to **86 253** and named *The Manchester Guardian - November 1980*) and eight coaches (including two Mark 2 SO's - seen here as second and third vehicles). In the view above, *Kolhapur* and its train pass beneath the intersection bridge south of Wigan Springs Branch MPD, where the former L&NWR Eccles, Tyldesley & Wigan route from Manchester via Platt Bridge, Hindley Green and Tyldesley can be seen converging on the main line immediately in front of the locomotive. Leaving Crewe at 11.11, the train was due to arrive in Preston at 12.17 where 'Britannia' BR Class 4-6-2 No **70032** *Tennyson* was booked as replacement for the climb over Shap to Carlisle (arr 14.34). Continuing over the 'Waverley' route into Scotland, LNER Class V2 2-6-2 No **60836** provided the motive power as far as Edinburgh Waverley (arr 17.18). Now in the hands of LNER Class A2 4-6-2 No **60532** *Blue Peter*, a four hour plus journey via Perth and Dundee would see arrival of the special in the 'Granite City' of Aberdeen (arr 21.31). The Sunday's schedule continues on page 10.....................   *Ray Farrell*

(Above) *Continued from page 9........Kolhapur* and its train that form the 'Granite City' Rail Tour come within sight of Springs Branch MPD. Built at Crewe in December 1934 and allocated to Crewe North (5A), *Kolhapur* was one of the 'Jubilees' to survive into preservation after withdrawal from Leeds Holbeck (55A) on 15th October 1967. On Sunday 4th September 1966, the rail tour returned to its schedule when LNER Class A4 4-6-2 No 60024 *Kingfisher* left Aberdeen at 10.10 for Edinburgh Waverley via Montrose and Dundee. Another four-hour spell, this time to York via Newcastle, was undertaken by another member of the A4 Class, this time No 60019 *Bittern*, a locomotive that would ultimately find itself subject to preservation. Diesel traction completed the mammoth tour with arrival back in London Kings Cross at 21.58.   *Ray Farrell*

Wigan Springs Branch on 3rd September 1966. Stanier Jubilee Class '6P5F' 4-6-0 No **45647** *Sturdee* heads a southbound passenger (Up relief) working 1T84 past Springs Branch No.1 Signal Box, whilst on the right an unidentified Stanier Class '8F' 2-8-0 backs under the coaling plant at the motive power depot (8F). *Sturdee* had worked relief (1X10) from Leeds to Blackpool the previous evening with a train which ran all Friday nights during the Illuminations.   It was due to return to Leeds on the Sunday so wherever the turn here was taking it would have to be fulfilled in time for the engine to return to Blackpool. The 'Jubilee' was built in January 1935 and initially allocated to Crewe North (5A). At this time it was based at Farnley Junction (55C) before withdrawal from Leeds Holbeck (55A) on 26th April 1967   *Ray Farrell*

BR Standard Class '9F' 2-10-0 No **92032** (8H - Birkenhead) heads a train load of coal 'empties' past Springs Branch on 3rd September 1966. No 1 Signal Box is to the left of picture – on the west (Down) side, with the motive power depot visible above the train. The '9F' is travelling along the freight only (Up East Goods) line, which gave access to Bamfurlong Sidings via a burrowing junction beyond Fir Tree House Junction Bridge. In this instance the lower calling on arm (of the bracket signal behind the locomotive) indicates to the driver that the signal ahead (Cromptons Sidings Home signal, lever 43) may be at danger but will be sufficient distance behind the train to clear the previous signals (on the Up East Goods) The freight is signalled to branch eastwards along the Manchester line, the junction being some 100 yards ahead. April 1967.   *Ray Farrell*

Royal Scot Class '7P' 4-6-0 No. **46168** *The Girl Guide* heads the Up 'Lakes Express' past Wigan Springs Branch MPD on 24th June 1961. The train also contained through carriages from Workington Main (which took the route via Keswick), whereas a Restaurant Car was provided on the Windermere portion (dep 10.50am SO - 11.5am during the week). The southbound working on Saturdays missed out calls at both Wigan and Warrington with a saving of twenty five minutes into Euston. On shed, BR Standard Class '5MT' 4-6-0 No. **73137** stands at the entrance letting off steam whilst on the right is Ex-LNW Class ''G2A''7F' 0-8-0 No. **49154**. The Scot was allocated to Preston (24K) at this time, having been introduced to traffic on 23rd October 1930 at Rugby and was withdrawn from Springs Branch (8F) during May 1964.   *Ray Farrell*

Brush type '4' (later Class 47) Co–Co diesel-electric **D1943** heads 1M37, the combined Aberdeen (dep 09.10) and Perth (dep 11.10) to Birmingham New Street past Wigan Springs Branch No 2 signal box on 3rd August 1966. The London Midland Region Timetable for the period indicates that the train had Through Carriages from Aberdeen. It was however a Saturdays Only working from 18th June to 3rd September. To illustrate how the four-position train identifications changed, the Working Timetable for 1961/62 shows 1M37 as the 12.15pm Perth to Euston train, the 'M' indicating that this was an Inter-Regional Train. Numbers were allocated by the corresponding Line Traffic Manager's (Line Control) Offices. Located between the Up Fast line and the Down East Goods lines, the 90 lever LMS frame all-timber box, situated 417 yds north of Springs Branch No 1 was closed on 1st october 1972. Under the T.O.P.S renumbering scheme, D1943 became **47 500** and subsequently named *Great Western* in 1979. It had been in traffic barely two months when it was photographed here at Wigan. To confuse matters, the loco was again renumbered 47 770 in May 1994 and renamed *Reserved*. **Ray Farrell**

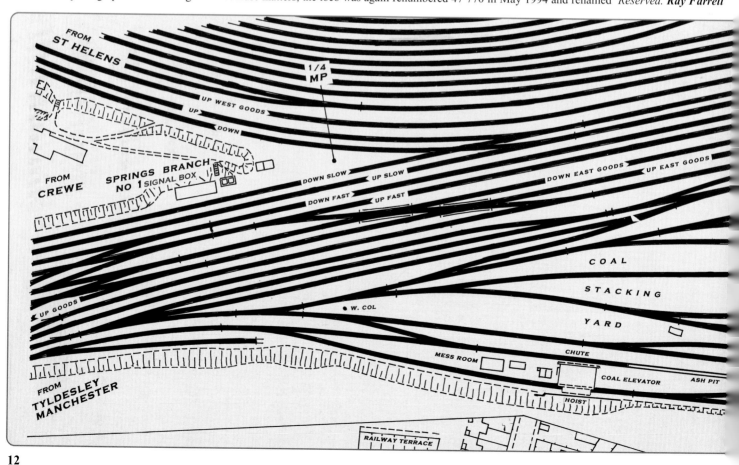

An unidentified Brush type '4' heads a southbound express past Wigan Springs Branch No 2 signal box on the Up Fast line, as a Stanier class '8F' 2-8-0 No **48379** commences its journey north with a 'mixed' Class 4 freight train on 25th August 1966, smokebox partially obliterated by a post full of shunting signals. Sister loco No **48319** also waits on the right and No 48319 was allocated to Springs Branch (8F) at this time, having been allocated to Perth (63A) when built in January 1944 and was withdrawn from Bolton (26C-9K) in June 1968.

Ray Farrell

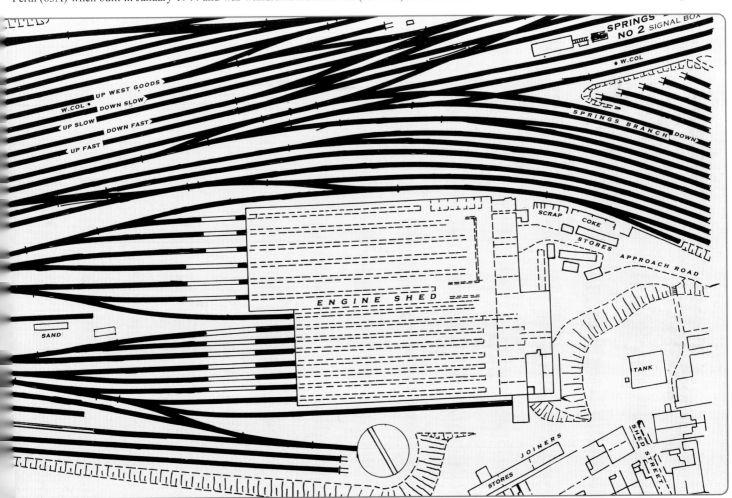

Springs Branch motive power depot, Wigan, on 24th June 1961. The shed code, now 8F, had been changed from 10A in 1958, thus ending an identity dating back as far as 1935. The 1958 reorganisation also placed Springs Branch under the control of Edge Hill (Liverpool - 8A). The facilities here comprised two main sheds of equal size, No 1, with eight roads and adjacent to the Springs Branch (as well as the Euston to Carlisle main line, dating from 1869. No 2 shed, also with eight roads, appeared in 1882, doubling the capacity at a stroke. Its motive power reflected the location of Springs Branch in a coal mining area and throughout the LMS and British Railways periods, the LNWR built 7F 0-8-0's reigned supreme until the final years of steam saw the infiltration of Class 5, both LMS and BR Standard types and 8F 2-8-0's. Traditional LNWR roofing styles which gave over eight decades of protection, were ultimately replaced although it was British Railways which defined the depot's final form. In the view above, the 'No 1' shed to the left contains a smattering of different loco types whilst to the right the LNWR 0-8-0 work horses occupy prime position. *Ray Farrell*

SPRINGS BRANCH
MOTIVE POWER DEPOT

The scenes shown here are those of the late Wallace Sutherland who, as a Chartered Engineer, came to these shores with his family in 1953 for an initial three year spell to expand his work experience. As it happened, Wallace stayed and spent the rest of his life here. One of his many shed visits throughout the UK took him on 23rd March 1963 to Springs Branch. The panoramic view covering the upper parts of this and the facing page shows the south elevation with 'No 1' shed to the left, still fully roofed, less than a decade after major reconstruction by British Railways. On this particular occasion, full details of the locomotives on shed were not recorded. However, some nine months earlier, a visit had seen the recording of no less than seventeen of the LNWR 0-8-0 7F's amongst the 56 engines on the depot. The 26th June 1962 'bash' revealed the following, all bearing 8F shed plates except those noted otherwise. *Fowler 2-6-4T Class 4* 42303; *Stanier 2-cyl Class 4T's* 42456/62/65; *Class 4F 0-6-0's* 44069, 44125, 44280, 44303, 44490, 44713 (5B); *Stanier Class 5MT 4-6-0's* 45107 (24F), 45108/09/35, 45281, 45294 (26F), 45313/14, 45341 (26A), 45372; *Patriot 4-6-0 Class 7P* 45521 *Rhyl* ; *Jubilee 4-6-0 Class 6P5F* 45604 *Ceylon* (24L); *Royal Scot 4-6-0 Class 7P's* 46161 *King's Own*, 46167 *The Hertfordshire Regiment;* *0-6-0T Class 3F* 47270, 47376 (8G), 47444, 47671 (no plate); *Stanier 2-8-0 Class 8F* 48017, 48742 (8A), 48756 (2A); *LNWR 0-8-0 Class 7F* No's 48895, 49008, 49025, 49104, 49122, 49129, 49139, 49141, 49154, 49267, 49314, 49344, 49381, 49408, 49447, 49451; *WD 'Austerity' 2-8-0 Class 8F* No's 90173, 90257, 90271 (26A), 90481 (56D), 90507; *British Railways 4-6-0 Standard Class 5* 73129 (26F); *BR Standard 2-6-0 Class 4* 76051; *BR Standard 2-6-0 Class 2* 78061;

(Right-lower) Transferred from Warrington in April of 1961, Stanier 2-cylinder Class 4 No **42607** would see out its days at Springs Branch, being withdrawn in February 1964, some eleven months after being photographed on shed. The loco could occasionally be seen on the Wigan Central to Manchester services although its withdrawal pre-dated the demise of the services on the former GC/CLC line.

Springs Branch shed was accessed from the Manchester (Eccles,Tyldesley & Wigan) line adjacent to Cromptons Sidings signal box. With the 'No 1' shed to our far left we get the opportunity to see the coal elevator and ash disposal area created in 1935 as part of the LMS motive power depot reorganisation. The 'No 2' shed had seen its covered area reduced by half but part of the site would however witness the construction of a new traction maintenance depot. This new facility would see numerous changes in function over the next three decades. The three locomotives in the foreground comprise (from right to left) WD 'Austerity 2-8-0 No **90574**, an engine that would see out its days at Springs Branch; Class 5MT 4-6-0 No's **44770** (5A - Crewe North) and **45191** (5D - Stoke).

J W Sutherland

Supposedly withdrawn before the end of 1962 from Newton Heath, Royal Scot Class No **46139** *The Welch Regiment* is posed for the camera at the end of the sand siding on 23rd March 1963, less the greater part of its motion with exterior beginning to look the worse for wear. It is reported by some sources as being stored in Newton Heath until April 1963 from where it was taken to Crewe Works (via Springs Branch?) for scrapping.

J W Sutherland

(**Right**) A busy scene around the coaling plant at Wigan Springs Branch MPD (8F) on 24th June 1961. Two ex-LNW Class G2a '7F' 0-8-0's No **49438** and No **49267** stand on the right, with Stanier Class '5' 4-6-0 No **45108** in front on the same track. A Stanier Class '8F' 2-8-0 No **48649**, unusually coupled with a Fowler straight sided tender, stands on the adjacent track. The two former LNW locomotives were withdrawn from Springs Branch on 30th and 27th November 1962 respectively. The Class '5' was also withdrawn from Springs Branch in December 1965, having been originally introduced to traffic at Crewe North (5A) on 22nd May 1935. The Stanier '8F' spent all its working life at Willesden (1A) other than a brief 2 month loan period to Rugby (2A-1F) at the end of 1947, and was withdrawn from its original base during February 1965, having been allocated there when built on 10th December 1943. *Ray Farrell*

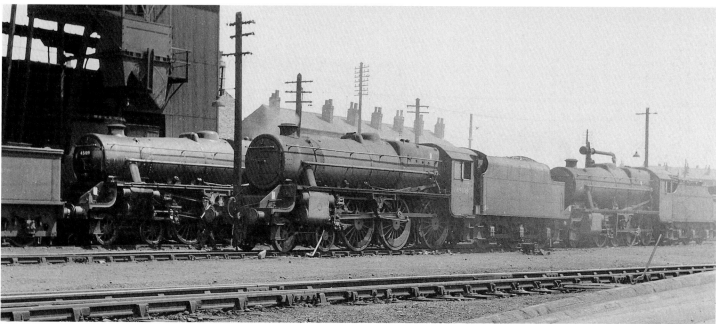

(**Above-centre**) Springs Branch MPD (8F) on 24th June 1961, with Stanier Class '5' 4-6-0's No **45109** against the coaling plant and sister loco No **45108** in front of Stanier Class '8F' 2-8-0 No **48649** on the adjacent line. No **45109**, at the time a Springs Branch loco, was withdrawn from Warrington Dallam (8B) during April 1967. *Ray Farrell*

(**Right**) Two Class J10 0-6-0 Nos. **65157** and **65198** stand silent at Springs Branch depot on 24th June 1961. Although they appear to be in externally poor condition, both locomotives have full tenders and presumably were available for use, although the former was recorded as withdrawn from Springs Branch on 23rd August 1961, just 8 weeks later. *Ray Farrell*

(Right) This fully coaled-up veteran of a Class first introduced in 1897 awaits its next turn of duty at Springs Branch on 16th April 1955. Built to a design by Barton-Wright and given the number 964 by the L&Y, **52051** gave its last years of active service to British Railways at the Wigan depot before being withdrawn in February 1956.   *C A Appleton*

SPRINGS BRANCH MPD

(Below) Ivatt Class '2' 2-6-0 No **46517** heads a southbound freight on the Up Slow line on 25th August 1966, having just passed beneath Cemetery Road bridge. The bridge, No 31, comprised spans of 49'-0" and 40'-6" respectively. The Ivatt, built in January 1953 and allocated to Oswestry (89A), had a working life of under 14 years, before withdrawal from Springs Branch (8F) during November 1966.   *Ray Farrell*

(Right) Before breaking our journey north to take a look at the Central Wagon Company's activities *(pages 20-22)*, we will move half a mile or so along the main line as far as Westwood Lane bridge (No 33). The south elevation shows the different type of construction used for bridging the four Fast lines (left) and the Goods lines (right). The small building to the right, the *British Energy Authority Sidings Frame* housed 10-levers to control access to and from the sidings serving Westwood Power Station, the two chimneys of which stand proud above the bridge parapets. Details of running lines and other information regarding this location is to be found beneath the north elevation photograph on *page 23.* This view was also recorded on 26th June 1963.

British Railways Board

CENTRAL WAGON COMPANY

The site at Ince was originally two separate concerns, namely the Central Wagon Company's works, situated on Manchester Road and Thompsons, whose establishment was at the side of the former Great Central station at Lower Ince. Both were accessed from the LNWR Springs Branch to the long closed Wigan Coal & Iron Company. Although the business was based primarily on the repair of wagons, along with some scrapping, it is known that LMS coaches were similarly dealt with - see page 22.

However, being one of the larger yards in the north-west capable of handling such work, the company began to take delivery of withdrawn locomotives in 1960, the Thompson yard being the first recipient. Long term however, only the Central Wagon site was operative by the mid-1960's. At least 313 locomotives are recorded as being cut up by the concern although CWC did have a site in Barrow so there is some confusion as to which site was responsible for cutting up which stock. From records kept by *Chris Coates* of 140 visits in the 1960's, most of those 313 scrapped engines are confirmed as being at Ince. One major query which has to this day not been resolved involves ex-GWR No 5015 *Dartmouth Castle*, which arrived at Springs Branch in the company of two GWR 'County' Class locos. This latter pair were later noted at Stockport Edgeley so the possibility remains that 5015's visit was part of a 'dropping off' exercise. Of the known engines cut up at CWC, arguably the most prestigious was 'Duchess' No 46243 *City of Lancaster (see title page)*, thought to have been inspected with a view to preservation. Other notable engines, including 'Scot' No 46129 *Scottish Horse,* eight 'Jubilees' and a rebuilt 'Patriot', 45522 *Prestatyn* were also victims of the cull. Some GWR locos did arrive, mainly Pannier tanks although two 'Halls' arrived in 1964, namely 4950 and 4976, the former almost immediately being cut up whilst the latter survived some four months. Former LNER locos passed through CWC including B1's, K3's and O2's. Things went very quiet on the locomotive side towards the end of 1965 and by the end of 1966 had almost ceased. The last recorded loco at the yard (C. Coates) was 78002 in February 1967.

(Right) Stanier Class '5MT' 2-6-0 'Mogul' No **42952** at Ince on 29th May 1965. The loco bears a chalked shed code of 8L, Aintree, although official records show 42952 as having moved to Springs Branch (8F) in July 1964 before withdrawal just three months later in September. Built in December 1935 and initially allocated to Kingmoor (Carlisle), the Stanier 'Crab' was withdrawn from Springs Branch during September 1964.

(Left-top) Not the gleaming machine seen on the title page but still retaining the majestic profile that Sir William A Stanier introduced some three decades earlier. However, now in the less auspicious surroundings at Lower Ince, 'Duchess' No **46243** *City of Lancaster* awaits its turn to be dismantled.

(Left-centre) Two of Stanier's finest - 'Jubilee' Class '6P5F' 4-6-0 No **45681** *Aboukir* and 'Princess Coronation' Class '8P' 4-6-2 No **46243** *City of Lancaster* stand somewhat ignominiously amongst the clutter of the breakers yard at Ince on 29th May 1965.

(Right-centre) More engines from the one-time LMS production line, on this occasion in the shape of two 'Derby 4's, still surprisingly attached to their respective tenders and photographed at CWC on 29th May 1965. Facing is No **44119**, which had latterly spent its time at Lower Darwen, had been withdrawn in December 1963. It was then stored at Springs Branch and is seen here barely a month before being cut up in June 1965. Its partner, No **44186,** had last seen its fire dampened at Barrow in October 1963. It remained stored there until August 1964 before being transferred to Lower Ince for the ultimate disposal.

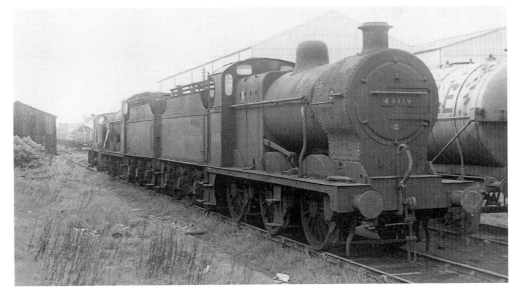

(Left-lower) Latterly based at Newton Heath, 'Jubilee' No **45623** *Palestine* forms an unlikely cab to cab configuration with WD 'Austerity' 2-8-0 No **90667**, one of over 700 of the class introduced to a design of 1943 and purchased by BR in 1948. 90667 had spent its last five years of active life at nearby Springs Branch, being withdrawn in May 1964.

(Right-lower) Stanier 2 – cylinder Class '4' 2-6-4T No **42481**, is seen still largely intact despite the surrounding debris, on 29th May 1965. Introduced to traffic at Nuneaton (2B-5E) on 10th February 1937, the loco spent its final eighteen years at Lostock Hall (24C-10D), being withdrawn from there during September 1964.

All: *Ray Farrell*

(Left) Thompson Class B1 4-6-0 No **61041**, built by the North British Loco Company in 1946, is most definitely in a poor state, indeed one wonders how the somewhat savage damage apparent to the footplate and cab side came about. If in model form it looks as though some large thumb has prized it from the box eagerly wanting to ru(i)n it. The loco was withdrawn from New England shed on 19th April 1964 and had spent its years mostly in the Eastern Counties with the exception of a week on the Southern Region in May 1953. Those halcyon days however are long gone and for this once proud Class, some bestowed with names such as *Springbok*, *Kudu*, and *Wildebeest,* the writing was on the wall.

(Right) There was little or no chance of escaping the breakers torch at CWC and none did; that was left to the flexible and forward thinking Dai Woodham at Barry in South Wales. As many as sixteen of the LNER Thompson designed Class B1 locomotives saw out their final days at Wigan, the pair here, No's **61056** and **61144** being but two that were condemned on the same day, 19th April 1964 and withdrawn and stored at Immingham shed. Both were less than twenty years old when scrapped during 1965.

(Left) The ultimate resting place of GW 'Hall' Class 4-6-0 No **4976** *Warfield Hall* would most certainly have baffled its original owners. In May 1964, prior to withdrawal, the loco had been based at Oxford following short spells at Didcot and Southall. Previous allocations during the mid-1950's saw this much travelled engine in the West Country and the depots at Plymouth Laira and Truro. Oxford to Wigan therefore was uncharted territory for its last journey, ending at Ince during the summer of 1965.

(Right) According to the identification chalked on the frame, this was all that remained of a once proud Stanier 'Jubilee' 4-6-0 No **45592** *Indore*, in the final stages of cutting up at Central Wagon Co. yard at Ince near Wigan on 29th May 1965. The Jubilee, allocated to Crewe North (5A) when first built in December 1934, had a wide variety of bases, most notably Camden (1B), where it spent most of the war years, returning there in June 1953 for another six years prior to withdrawal from Newton Heath (26A-9D) during September 1964. Evidence of the reports that LMS coaching stock was cut up on site is confirmed in this somewhat apocalyptic scenario.   All: *Ray Farrell*

Wigan, 26th June 1963. With Springs Branch receding into the distance, this view south through the openings of Westwood Lane bridge (No 33) allow us the opportunity to view the high speed alignment of the running lines on the approach to Wigan. Maximum permissible speed on Main and Fast lines between Crewe and Gretna Junction was 90mph although crews on expresses from the south were by now preparing for the 50mph restriction that was in force over the curves north and south of North Western station. In this view, from left to right, lines were designated as follows:- Up and Down East Goods; Up and Down Fast; Up and Down Slow. The small wooden building of L&NWR origin - no doubt relocated from elsewhere - to the right was the *British Energy Authority Sidings Frame* and contained 10 levers controlling access to and from the sidings serving Westwood Power Station of the North West Electricity Board. A Private Siding Agreement had only been granted to the Central Electricity Generating Board some three years earlier which probably explains the presence of a two-road engine shed adjacent to the power station.　　　　　　*British Railways Board*

CHAPTER TWO
ONWARDS TO WIGAN (NORTH WESTERN) STATION

Heading north away from Springs Branch the Euston to Glasgow (WCML) route passed under three bridges in quick succession. Bridge No.31 – Cemetery Road with two spans of 49'-0"(over the Down and Up Slow lines as well as the Down and Up Fast) and 40'-6" (which spanned the Down and Up East Goods as well as the truncated remains of the line serving the erstwhile Orchard Colliery). Intersection bridge No.32 – carrying the L&YR Pemberton Loop (Pemberton Junction - Hindley No 2; closed to passengers 14.7.69) over spans of 8'-0", 32'-0" and 75'-0" respectively, the line enabling Wigan Wallgate to be be avoided. At Pemberton Junction, the original route to Liverpool Exchange, the *Liverpool, Bolton and Bury Railway* would head west through Orrell, Rainford Junction and Fazackerley towards Merseyside. Bridge No.33 (Westwood Lane - seen in the foreground above) with spans of 26'-0" (over the Down and Up Slow lines) and 48'-0" (over the Down and Up Fast lines and Down and Up East Goods lines respectively).

Approaching North Western Station, Westwood Power Station dominated the skyline on the west side of the railway. Commissioned in 1951 it was supplied with coal either by rail from adjacent Westwood sidings or by barge via the Leeds and Liverpool Canal which passed beneath the line immediately north of the power station. This was closed in the early 1980's and completely demolished in 1989.

To the east of the main line approaching North Western Station the former L&Y line from Manchester and Bolton via Ince converged alongside before dropping sharply to access Wigan Wallgate Station and thence to Liverpool/Southport.

Situated between the Up East Goods line and the Down Manchester line and some 1,547 yards north of Springs Branch No. 2 was Wigan No.1 signal box. Built in 1941 to wartime specifications the brick structure housed two frames, an 85 - lever Western frame and a 40 - lever Central frame. It was closed on 1st October 1972 following commissioning of the Weaver Junction to Glasgow resignalling scheme.

Wigan North Western Station, occupying the site where the N.U. opened its original Wigan terminus at Chapel Lane on 3rd September 1832, had by the 1960's five through platforms supplemented by 4 southern bays and a single northern bay. The main lines used platform 2 (Up) and platform 3 (Down) whilst bay 5 at the northern end was used for trains to Blackburn via the L.U. line at Boars Head. Passenger traffic on this route ceased from the 4th January 1960.

At the northern end of the station the line crossed Wallgate thoroughfare (Bridge No.43). *The Swan & Railway*, a welcome haunt for photographers in those heady days of main line steam, stood almost beneath the bridge and remains still albeit now dispensing Banks' Bitter.

Wigan No.2 signal box, situated 792 yards north of No.1 box between the Down Main line and the westerly carriage sidings was also a wartime structure, housed a 65-lever frame and also met its demise 1st October 1972.

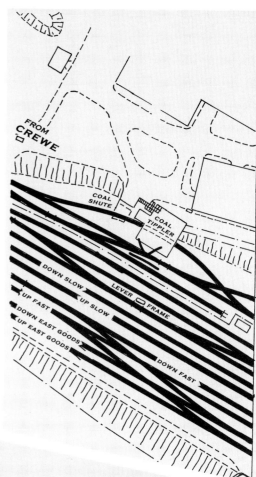

(**Above**) A sunny day in Wigan, 26th June 1963 as children stroll and mothers push their prams along an otherwise quiet Westwood Lane, no doubt oblivious to the trains that may be passing a few feet below. *BR(LMR)*

Royal Scot Class '7P' 4-6-0 No **46126** *Royal Army Service Corps* passes Westwood Power Station as it heads south with 1G14 the 8.20am Carlisle – Birmingham New Street on 24th June 1961. The train also had Through Carriages from both Workington Main and Whitehaven the connection via Barrow being made at Lancaster. The 'Scot' was based at Willesden (1B) at this time and was withdrawn whilst at Annesley (16D-16B) by early October 1963. The power station, commissioned in 1951, fared little better, being closed in the early 1980's and totally demolished during 1989. *Ray Farrell*

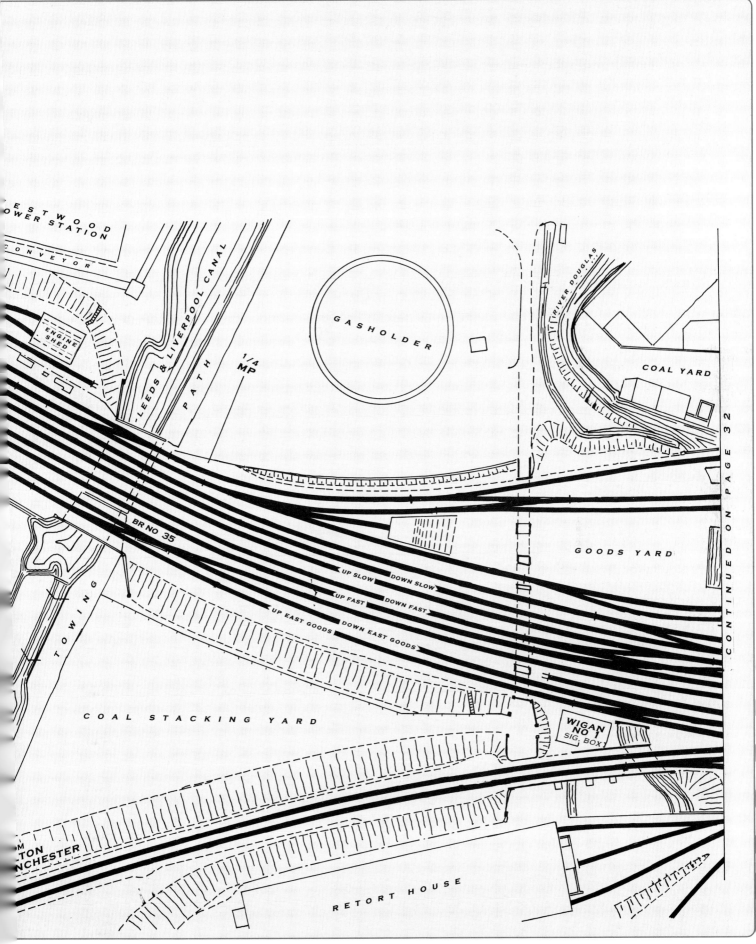

WESTWOOD
POWER STATION

CONVEYOR

ENGINE
SHED

LEEDS & LIVERPOOL CANAL

PATH

1/4
MP

GASHOLDER

RIVER DOUGLAS

COAL YARD

BR NO 35

TOWING

UP SLOW   DOWN SLOW
UP FAST   DOWN FAST
UP EAST GOODS   DOWN EAST GOODS

GOODS YARD

COAL STACKING YARD

WIGAN
NO 1
SIG. BOX

FROM
BOLTON
MANCHESTER

RETORT HOUSE

CONTINUED ON PAGE 32

(**Above**) With the main line rails glistening in the foreground, Stanier Class '4' 2-6-4T No **42644** of Wigan Springs Branch (8F) pilots Newton Heath's (26A-9D) Stanier Class '5' 4-6-0 No **45224** at the head of the 12.45pm (SO) Manchester Victoria to Southport Chapel Street as it approaches Wigan Wallgate (arr 1.12pm) on the former L&Y route to make one of only two intermediate stops (the other was Southport St Lukes) en-route on its 53 minute scheduled journey. The date is the 28th May 1960.

(**Left**) British Railways Standard Class 4 2-6-0 No **76075**, with a rather 'mixed' freight in tow, will shortly transfer from the Down East Goods (NU) line onto the Down Lostock to Pemberton line, a manoeuvre which will take it through Wigan Wallgate and on to Liverpool for the docks. This 28th May 1960 view shows a consignment of MG 'MGA' cars on their way from Abingdon (Oxon) to Liverpool for the American market. Note the 'white-wall tyres' and the over-riders on the bumpers, a requirement of the US market. The locomotive, built in December 1956, was initially allocated to Sutton Oak (8G) and was withdrawn from Wigan Springs Branch (8F) after a working life of less than 11 years on 5th October 1967. Both; *Ray Farrell*

With Westwood Power Station dominating the background. Stanier Jubilee 4-6-0 No **45738** *Samson*, at the head of the 12.8pm ex-Crewe to Blackpool Central (arr 2.38pm) train, passes an unidentified 'WD' Class '8F' 2-8-0 heading freight south over the Leeds & Liverpool Canal, just south of Wigan North Western on 28th May 1960. The passenger working started the day as the 8.20am London Euston to Liverpool Lime Street, with through carriages (TC) from Crewe - where the train was split - to Blackpool. The Jubilee, built in November 1936, was at this time an Upperby (12B) loco and moved to Kingmoor (12A) in 1962, being withdrawn from the Carlisle depot during December 1963.

Ray Farrell

A stirring sight indeed as the eponymous Stanier Princess Royal Class '8P' 4-6-2 No **46200** brings a Birmingham to Glasgow/Edinburgh train through the curves south of Wigan North Western station on 28th May 1960. This working, non-stop between Crewe (dep 12.34pm) and Carlisle (arr 3.23pm), had left Birmingham New Street at 10.55am and had Restaurant Car facilities throughout to Glasgow. First port of call en-route was Wolverhampton, followed by Stafford. After Carlisle, a very efficient splitting of the train was carried out at Carstairs where the Edinburgh (Princes Street) portion departed (5.5pm) some two minutes after the main train had left, first for Motherwell and then Glasgow (arr 5.47pm). *The Princess Royal* was built in June 1933 and had a nomadic existence, being allocated to Crewe North, Camden, Upperby, Edge Hill, Polmadie and Camforth before withdrawal from Carlisle Kingmoor (12A) during November 1962.

Ray Farrell

Saturday 28th May 1960 certainly brought about a unique double in more ways than one. Following the first member of the Princess Royal Class (46200) within a matter of minutes was the unique British Railways Class '8P' 4-6-2 No **71000** *Duke of Gloucester*, seen here approaching Wigan with the 9.50am ex-London Euston to Perth train. The time would be approximately 1.50pm, with passengers of this anglo-scottish service facing a further five hours before arrival in Perth (arr 7.13pm). Since the previous November, the train had been rescheduled following the effects of Main Line Electrification work south of Crewe where line occupation had become a premium. The improved timings came as a result of reverting to the previous weekday times, with a saving of about twenty minutes. Built in May 1954 the BR Pacific lasted only $8\frac{1}{2}$ years, spent mainly at Crewe North (5A) from where it was withdrawn on 24th November 1962. Initially destined for the national collection as a result of several unique features, the locomotive, less numerous important components, was banished to Barry Docks where it languished for over six years. Following the efforts of the Duke of Gloucester Steam Locomotive Trust, 71000, with many major improvements, steamed again in 1986 and has since enjoyed a happy renaissance on Britain's railways, particularly the Great Central Railway at Loughborough.

Ray Farrell

Against a background of gasometers, chimneys and church spires, Stanier Class '5' 4-6-0 No **44847** takes advantage of the advantageous descent away from Wigan on the Up Fast line with mixed goods train on 25th August 1966. Above the engine is the flat roofed engine shed serving Westwood Power Station whilst to the far right, immediately in front of the small gasometer, on the right is Wigan No 1 signal box, commissioned in 1941 when the signalling in the area was modernised. The Class '5' was built in August 1945 and allocated to Southport (27C-8M). It then spent a short time at Aintree (27B-8L) and was withdrawn whilst at Kingmoor during December 1967.

Ray Farrell

(Left) A pair of Crewe North (5A) locos, Class '2P' 4-4-0 No **40655** and Stanier Jubilee Class No **45684** *Jutland*, double head a Workington – Euston train southwards, having just passed through Wigan North Western station on 13th August 1958, one of three such summer Saturday trains which gave the Cumberland town through carriage facilities to London and an opportunity to view parts of the Lake District via the scenic line through Keswick. Built in February 1936, *Jutland* was to last until December 1965 when it was withdrawn from Bank Hall (27A-8K). Its companion was not so fortunate, being withdrawn from its Crewe base during November 1959.

Ray Farrell

(Above) **Running to express train scheduling,** Stanier Class '5' 4-6-0 No **44926**, a Liverpool Edge Hill (8A) loco, heads a southbound train of (probably) empty assorted utility vans and non-passenger coaching stock along the Up Fast line away from Wigan North Western station on 29th May 1965. About to pass over the Leeds & Liverpool Canal (Br No 35), we get a reminder of Wigan's recent past power requirements with the gas holder, above the engine and hemmed in by the canal and the River Douglas, the latter flowing beneath the railway adjacent to the No 1 signal box which is to the extreme right of the picture. The Class '5', built in February 1946, spent all its working life in the north west, moving from Southport, to Blackpool, Bolton, Patricroft, Newton Heath, Lancaster, and finally to Edge Hill (8A) from where it was withdrawn during April 1968.

Ray Farrell

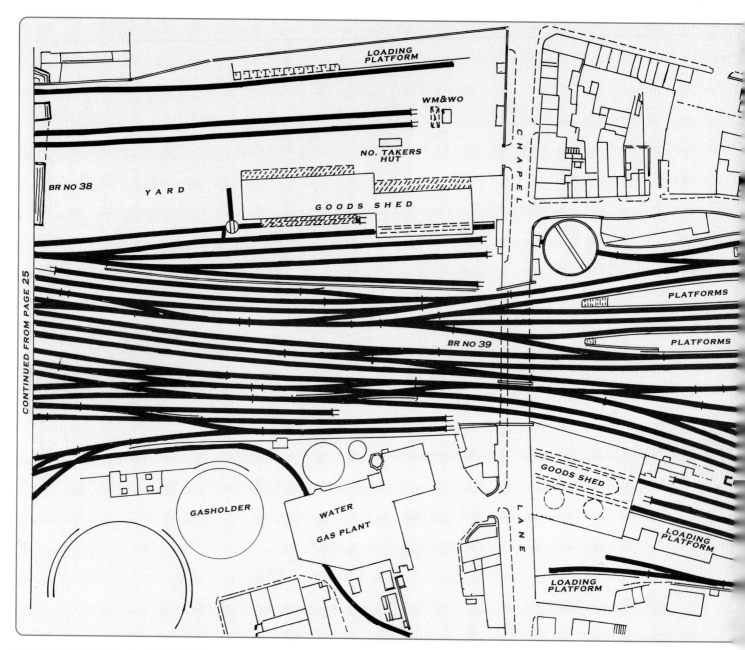

LOADING PLATFORM

WM&WO

NO. TAKERS HUT

BR NO 38

YARD

GOODS SHED

CHAPEL

PLATFORMS

PLATFORMS

BR NO 39

CONTINUED FROM PAGE 25

GOODS SHED

LANE

LOADING PLATFORM

GASHOLDER

WATER GAS PLANT

LOADING PLATFORM

CONTINUED ON PAGE 42

(**Left-opposite**) The Wigan North Western of yesteryear is remembered in this view taken on Saturday 19th May 1923 of 'Jumbo' 2-4-0 No **787** *Clarendon* awaiting departure with 4.7pm train to Manchester Exchange from the Up bay platform at the southern end of the station. From LNWR days until withdrawal of the service in 1964 there had been a requirement for a late afternoon service. Arrival in Manchester was destined to vary marginally between 5.15 and 5.30pm. Generally this was adhered to but as unremunerative intermediate stations closed, particularly pre-Beeching, departure from Wigan was gradually put back, nominally to around 4.15 approx; However, the train here would include in its 58 minute journey the stations at Platt Bridge, Hindley Green, Howe Bridge and Tyldesley where a two minute stop was allowed. Leaving Tyldesley at 4.31pm, the longest unbroken distance between stations (3³/4 miles) to Ellenbrook (for Boothstown) would be followed by a series of calls at seven stations with less than a mile between them, namely Worsley (4.42pm), Monton Green (4.45), Eccles 4.48, Weaste 4.52, Seedley (4.54), Cross Lane (4.57), and Ordsall Lane, for Salford (5.0). Arrival in Manchester Exchange was scheduled for 5.9pm;

Authors collection

33

(Above) Royal Scot Class '7P' 4-6-0 No **46159** *The Royal Air Force* approaches Wigan North Western station with a train for Windermere -Whitehaven -Workington on 5th July 1958. The train, due to arrive in Wigan at 12.7pm, contained through carriages for Whitehaven Bransty and Workington Main via Barrow in Furness. The 'Scot' was introduced to traffic at Rugby (2A-1F) on 13th August 1930, and based at Crewe North (5A) at the time of the photograph. The loco was withdrawn from Willesden (1A) on 25th November 1962. *Ray Farrell*

Crewe North's (5A) Stanier Princess Coronation Class '8P' 4-6-2 No **46253** *City of St Albans* takes the 50mph speed resriction in its stride on the the southern approaches to North Western station with a Birmingham – Glasgow train on 24th January 1959. Important changes to the LMR Passenger Services Timetable had taken place in recent months due to the onset of the Main Line Electrification scheme, principally affecting the services between London Euston,Glasgow and Perth amongst others. It was also stated that principalAnglo-Scottish day services would in some cases be speeded up, particularly the 'Royal Scot'. This Birmingham to Glasgow (RC and TC to Glasgow, TC to Edinburgh) service however suffered somewhat in that the over al journey time was increased by forty-five minutes to over six and a half hours. The 4-6-2, a post-war locomotive, was allocated to Camden (1B) when new in September 1946 and withdrawn from Crewe North (5A) on 23rd January 1963, a working life of just over 16 years. *Ray Farrel*

Built in June 1933, Princess Royal Class '8P' 4-6-2 No **46200** *The Princess Royal* was the first of the twelve Stanier designed pacifics which preceded the Princess Coronation Class introduced in 1937. The Crewe North (5A) based loco is passing through Wigan North Western's platform 2 with a Glasgow/Edinburgh – Birmingham New Street express on 21st September 1959 and looking totally comfortable with its lengthy train. Although not quite running in the 'slipstream' of the "Royal Scot", this working kept a similarly timed non-stop schedule on its journey south, arriving at Crewe but fifteen minutes after its illustrious forerunner, despite having left Glasgow barely five minutes later. No doubt the ten minutes at Carstairs for the connection with the Edinburgh portion and a stop at Carlisle ate into the timetable to give for an otherwise speedy journey between England and Scotland, albeit only as far as Crewe. The engine was withdrawn from Carlisle Kingmoor (12A) just over three years later during November 1962. The wooden structure visible above the loco housed a hoist, used to convey perishables to platform 3 which housed a connecting facility. Visible to the far right is the footbridge, which spanned both the former L&Y goods and coal yard and the former L&Y lines into which descended into Wigan Wallgate station.   *Ray Farrell*

Standing at the southern end of platform 2 , Stanier Jubilee Class '6P5F' 4-6-0 No **45558** *Kashmir* prepares to take water on 7th June 1958. Based at Upperby (12B) at this time, the Jubilee moved to Kingmoor (12A) during July 1962 and was withdrawn from the Carlisle depot during week ending 1st May 1965. Although there were numerous train movements involving Carlisle engines around the Wigan area, it has not been possible to in this instance to identify the reason for *Kashmir's* presence in the station. Still carrying the headlamp code for an ordinary passenger or mixed train unfortunately does not help but then it was not unknown for other depots to 'borrow' engines, officially or otherwise, causing widespread confusion amongst both official and the enthusiasts fraternity.   *Ray Farrell*

WIGAN WALLGATE

Bury shed's (26D-9M) Stanier 2-cylinder Class '4' 2-6-4T No **42444** departs Wigan Wallgate with the 11.55am (Saturdays Only) Southport (Chapel Street) to Rochdale (arr 1.38pm) on 28th May 1960. Due to depart Wigan at 12.43pm, the overall journey would average a creditable 35mph, giving the passenger a leisurely one hour, forty three minutes across both agricultural and industrial Lancashire. Being a Bury 'turn', the engine would be prepared and ready to leave Bury shed between 7.45 and 8.00am. One time Bury fireman George Ellis recalls this working, driver Fred Heap regularly at the controls. Stations en-route on this cross country ramble included the now long closed St Lukes (Southport), Bradley Fold, Radcliffe Black Lane, Bury Knowsley Street, Broadfield and Heywood, although the latter reappeared in a later reincarnation as a single platform serving the East Lancashire Railway. Wallgate station, which stood virtually at a right angle to its main line neighbour, served the former L&Y routes to Southport and Liverpool Exchange, the lines passing under the Euston - Glasgow route just a short distance from Wallgate. The loco moved to Bolton (26C-9K) during September 1962 where it was noted that the footplate and cab fittings were in good clean condition, an ex-Bolton shed man being convinced that the engine, which spent much of its time as 'pilot' at Rochdale when allocated to Bury, was called upon so infrequently that the crew had nothing else to do but keep their working area in good order. It was withdrawn from Bolton during May 1964.

Ray Farrell

At the south end of the town, or Wallgate to be more precise, Wallgate and North Western stations lived almost side by side. In fact, on numerous occasions the timetables requested passengers to walk between the two stations to effect a connection. The view here, taken from the higher level Euston to Glasgow line at a point where the L&NWR and L&YR formed an intersection (Bridge No 44 on the North Union, No 49 on the Lostock to Pemberton Line) shows Wallgate's island platform looking in the direction of Bolton and Manchester. The platforms to the right provide a loading facility for wagons, etc., whilst a row of single storey buildings to the extreme right served as the railways own Works Department. Leaving Wigan with a stopping train from Manchester Victoria (via the Atherton Line), the Saturdays Only 1.7pm departure is unidentified 'Crab' 2-6-0 with a four coach train. During the week, the service called at all stations between Wigan and Southport. On Saturdays only, St lukes became the first call after Wallgate. *Ray Farrell*

(Left) Memories are made of this! A trainspotters delight sees youngsters on both platforms obtain the perfect position to follow their hobby. Leeds Holbeck (55A) Jubilee Class '6P5F' 4-6-0 No **45565** *Victoria* waits alongside platform 3 at Wigan with a Blackpool bound train on 7th June 1958. This was the last Saturday of the 'Winter' Passenger Services Timetable and in all probability this was an ex-London Euston to Crewe train with through carriages to Blackpool Central. Restaurant Car facilities were available to Crewe and thence the service was advertised as through carriages from Crewe to Blackpool, change at Kirkham for Fleetwood. Built in August 1934, the Jubilee began its working life at Preston (24K) and ended it some 32½ years later when withdrawn from Low Moor (56F) on 6th January 1967.   *Ray Farrell*

Wigan North Western's platform 2 appears to have been taken over by the builders as Stanier Jubilee Class '6P5F' 4-6-0 No **45560** *Prince Edward Island*, an Edge Hill (8A) loco at this time, draws draws to a halt with a southbound passenger working, on 13th August 1958. In common with many stations of the former L&NWR, it was possible to see how the station had developed over the years. From its Wigan Branch days when the station entrance was a short distance south of Wallgate bridge, the redevelopment to enlarge the station on a substantial scale affected both sides of the original alignment, the Down side, with substantial retaining walls, more than the Up although work to the latter (platform 1 side) was sufficient to eliminate the original entrance, to be replaced by typical unpretentious L&NWR 'hole in the wall', with similarities to Stockport or Rugby where the railway was constructed above the natural ground contours and entrance was via a (dismal) subway. The development of the station south of Wallgate in the 1870's made sure that passenger protection from the elements was comprehensive. However, the platform canopies and roofing would ultimately suffer from settlement. The transverse trusses of the canopies were of a fairly lightweight nature compared with heavily engineered facilities elsewhere and the photographs on this page illustrate the difficulties of maintenance, especially after WW2 and lack of financial resources to replace them. These days, one is likely to be less of a victim to the weather without overhead protection as one would be from deteriorating canopies of 'steam' days. The Jubilee, built in July 1934, was to survive until the end of November 1963 when withdrawn from Crewe North (5A).   *Ray Farrell*

Last but one day before the introduction of the Summer timetable, the 9.0am ex-Perth to Euston, headed by Stanier Princess Coronation Class '8P' 4-6-2 No **46229** *Duchess of Hamilton*, passes alongside platform 2 at Wigan North Western, on 7th June 1958. Once again, the 50mph restriction on the approaches either side of Wigan will see a cautious passing through the station, giving enthusiasts such as the one on the left time to admire the 'Duchess'. This undoubtedly long train also called at Preston on its journey south to pick up the through carriages from Workington Main (dep 10.50am) and Whitehaven which had been worked around the Cumbrian coast via Barrow. For hardier souls, the train departing from Inverness at 11.20pm the night before was scheduled to make the connection at Perth. The Pacific had moved on to Camden by the time of this photo, and was withdrawn from Edge Hill (8A) in February 1964, fortunately to be preserved. Built in September 1938 as one of the twenty-four streamlined members of the Class, *Duchess of Hamilton* was sent to the United States, in conjunction with the World's Fair, at the start of 1939 in the guise of 6220 *Coronation.* Due to WW2, it did not return until February 1942, its original identity being restored. The streamlined casing was removed in 1948, giving it the appearance seen here. Following withdrawal, it was subsequently purchased for display at Butlins, Minehead where it remained until 1976 when, under a loan arrangement it was transferred to the National Railway Museum, York. It was restored to service in 1980 by the Friends of the NRM and operated until

1985. Following another period involving extensive renovation, 6229 returned to main line service in 1989 until 1996. However, the story does not end there, for following support by the Friends of the NRM and readers of Steam Railway magazine to see a return of the engine to its original condition, the loco was transferred to the Birmingham Railway Museum at Tyseley where the streamlined casing was to be manufactured, the aim being to return the Duchess to York in 2007 for the 70th Anniversary of the 'Coronation Scot' service. *Ray Farrell*

(Right) After closure in March 1952 of Lower Ince shed, the allocation of former Great Central Class 9H 0-6-0 engines were transferred to Springs Branch. Reclassified as J10 by the LNER, the company renumbered the engine 5118 in 1924 and stayed as such until 1946, when it became 5192. Under British Railways, the engine received its final identity, 65192. Here she stands at North Western station's platform 4 during a lull in pilot duties on 13th June 1959. Built at Gorton in 1902, the loco was withdrawn on 11th May 1960 after nearly six decades of service. *Ray Farrell*

(Right) Amidst delapidation and decay of the station platforms, Crewe North's (5A) Royal Scot Class 7P' 4-6-0 No **46134** *The Cheshire Regiment* draws W179, the 11.45am ex-London Euston to Whitehaven and Workington Main via Barrow, alongside Wigan North Western's platform 3 on 7th June 1958. Five minutes were allowed at Wigan (arr 3.50pm), followed by calls at Preston (arr 4.20pm), Lancaster (arr 4.54pm) and Carnforth (arr 5.15pm). From here onwards it really was time "to sit back and enjoy the scenery" as it would take over three hours, inclusive of calls at another twenty five stations to reach the final destination (24 unless one wanted to alight at Drigg which required notice to be given to the Guard at Ravenglass). A Restaurant Car was provided between Euston and Crewe with the remainder of the journey to West Cumberland advertised as through carriages. The 'Scot' was allocated to 5A when built in 1927 and survived in re-built form until withdrawn from Upperby (12B) on 27th November 1962. *Ray Farrell*

(Above) Manchester's Newton Heath Jubilee Class '6P5F' 4-6-0 No **45701** *Conqueror,* carrying express headcode, runs alongside platform 3 with a Manchester Victoria/Exchange to Glasgow train on 7th June 1958. This working had a long history, originating in LNWR days with a 4.15 pm departure from Manchester Exchange, in fact the July 1922 timetable shows the train calling at Eccles and Tyldesley prior to Wigan. There were also through carriages to Windermere included. During WW2, departure time from Exchange was adjusted to 4.5pm, reverting to the earlier schedule after cessation of hostilities. Moving on however to post-nationalisation days, the train commenced its journey from Manchester Victoria platform 11 middle/Exchange platform 3 and was known to the Newton Heath staff and crews as the 'Afternoon Scot', again with a 4.15pm departure and running via Ordsall Lane Junction, Eccles, Monton Green, Tyldesley and Springs Branch Junction to Wigan North Western. The 1958 timetable points out that Restaurant Car and Through Carriages served the Manchester-Glasgow portion whilst Through Carriages from Liverpool Exchange to Glasgow and Edinburgh were attached at Preston. The Newton Heath engine, well 'coaled up' at this stage, and crew, worked the train through to Glasgow. *Ray Farrell*

THE CALEDONIAN

Camden's (1B) Stanier Princess Coronation Class '8P' 4-6-2 No **46239** *City of Chester* runs alongside platform 2 with the Up morning "Caledonian" on a wet and dismal 13th August 1958. Departing Glasgow Central at 8.30am – Monday to Friday only – the Restaurant Car expresses - there were morning and afternoon versions during the summer of 1958 only - offered a full breakfast for 7/6d (37½ p), whilst dinner in the First Class cost 12/6d (62½p), but only 10/6d (52½p) in Second. Due in Euston at 3.45pm (later to become 3.35 pm), the morning express, with just one stop at Carlisle, was scheduled to cover the 401¼ mile journey in 7 hours 15 minutes, an average speed of 55mph. The "Caledonian", introduced during the summer of 1957 by the London Midland and Scottish Regions proved to be relatively short lived affair, being

withdrawn by 1964 as electrification between Crewe and Euston saw a reduction in train services. The eight coach train comprised six BR standard vehicles with the Kitchen car and a Brake first of LMS origin. For the rest of its life, the "Caledonian" reverted to one Up and one Down working each day. The Pacific, built in August 1939, spent over 21 years of its 25 year life span at Camden and was withdrawn from Crewe North (5A) during September 1964.

Ray Farrell

Stanier Princess Coronation Class '8P' 4-6-2 No **46255** *City of Hereford* is about to pass over Wallgate bridge and alongside platform 2 with a southbound express on 5th July 1958. The descent from Boars Head Junction at a predominent 1 in 104 gradient for nearly two miles, coupled with a 45 chain heavily canted curve into the station, reduced the mightiest of machines to what would appear a crawl (50mph restriction). Built in October 1946 and allocated new to Camden (1B), the pacific was at this time a Carlisle Upperby (12B) engine and was withdrawn from Carlisle Kingmoor (12A) during September 1964.

Ray Farrell

(Right) On the penultimate day of the 'winter' timetable (*16th September 1957 to 8th June 1958*) Crewe North's (5A) Stanier Princess Coronation Class No **46253** *City of St Albans* at the head of a combined Glasgow/Edinburgh – Birmingham train on 7th June 1958. With a payload of some 12/13 carriages in tow, the service offered Restaurant Car (RC) facilities on the Glasgow portion and (TC) through carriage(s) to Plymouth (North road), also from Glasgow. With connections at Crewe with the Liverpool/ Manchester composition for Cardiff, there was a need for some good timekeeping. Allocated to Camden (1B) when built in September 1946, the Pacific finished its days at its Crewe base, being withdrawn on 23rd January 1963.

(Centre) Photographed from the same spot, Rebuilt Patriot Class '7P' 4-6-0 No **45532** *Illustrious* approaches the station at the head of a southbound express (Reporting Number W545) on 7th June 1958. As in the view above, there is further evidence of the Wigan power signalling scheme of 1941, one of numerous schemes planned by the LMS but interrupted by WW2. Note also the roof profile of the ARP brick and concrete Wigan No 2 signal box. Built in April 1933, the Patriot was at this time a Camden (1B) loco, and was withdrawn from Carlisle Upperby (12B) during week ending 1st February 1964.

(Right-lower) Rounding the north curve into Wigan North Western on 24th January 1959, past Wigan No 2 signal box, with the Up "Royal Scot", rebuilt Fowler 4-6-0 No **46125** *3rd Carabinier* provides unusual motive power for this working. To generations the train was the preserve of the "Duchess" or Princess Coronation Class locomotive so one can almost hear the cries of surprise, perhaps indignation, at the sight of one of the lesser mortals on such a prestige train. The "Royal Scot" recieved its 'name' in 1927, and became one of the most notable trains on Britain's railways. In 1954, the service dropped it's Through Carriage facility, concentrating on Glasgow. It had become one of the early recipients of the new BR standard coaching stock, comprising 13 vehicles. By coincidence, the loco seen here built in 1927, was based at Crewe North (5A) at this time, and was withdrawn from Annesley (16D-16B), after a spell on the Great Central main line, during week ending 3rd October 1964. Official records indicate that 46125 was reallocated no less than 39 times, including loan periods, during its 37 year career, seventeen of them involving a return to Crewe North where it all began.

All (3); *Ray Farrell*

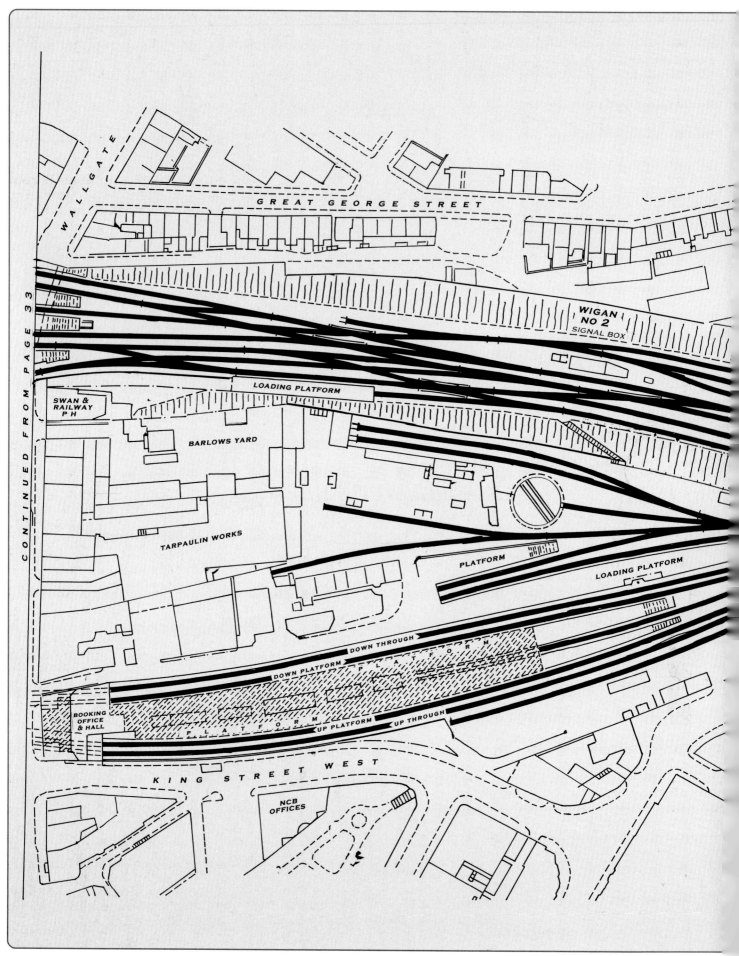

GREAT GEORGE STREET

WALLGATE

CONTINUED FROM PAGE 33

WIGAN NO 2 SIGNAL BOX

LOADING PLATFORM

SWAN & RAILWAY P H

BARLOWS YARD

TARPAULIN WORKS

PLATFORM

LOADING PLATFORM

DOWN THROUGH

DOWN PLATFORM

PLATFORM

BOOKING OFFICE & HALL

UP PLATFORM

UP THROUGH

KING STREET WEST

NCB OFFICES

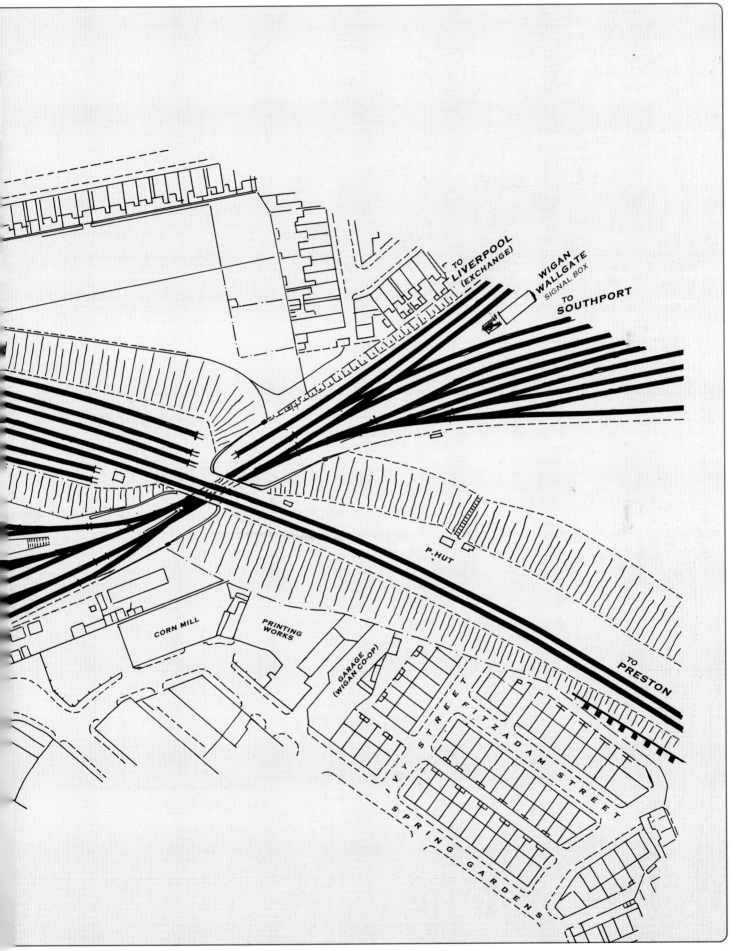

TO
LIVERPOOL
(EXCHANGE)

WIGAN
WALLGATE
SIGNAL BOX

TO
SOUTHPORT

P. HUT

CORN MILL

PRINTING
WORKS

GARAGE
(WIGAN CO-OP)

TO
PRESTON

FITZADAM STREET

STREET

SPRING GARDENS

FAREWELL TO
WIGAN

(Right) Departing North Western station's platform 3 is Stanier 'Jubilee' 4-6-0 No **45653** *Barham* with a train for Blackpool on 13th June 1959. On this occasion, the penultimate day of the 'winter' timetable *(15th September 1958 to 14th June 1959)*. The Jubilee, built in January 1935, was based primarily in the north west. At this time it was a Blackpool engine (24E-10B), and was finally withdrawn from Newton Heath (26A-9D) during week ending 3rd April 1965.

(Centre) Royal Scot Class '7P' 4-6-0 No **46136** *The Border Regiment*, waits to depart from Wigan North Western's platform 3 with a London (Euston) – Workington train on 7th June 1958. Built in 1927 and allocated to Crewe North (5A), 46136 spent more than thirty years of its 36$\frac{1}{2}$ year working life at Carlisle Upperby, before withdrawal from 12B during March 1964.

(Below) Stanier Jubilee Class '6P5F' 4-6-0 No **45588** *Kashmir* heads a northbound express freight, bound for Carlisle Canal Yard, through Wigan North Western on 13th June 1959. This was the penultimate day of the frieght working timetable and the working did not appear in the arrangements that were to follow. Built in December 1934, the Jubilee entered service at Crewe North (5A), was at this time an Upperby (12B) engine and was withdrawn from Kingmoor (12A) during week ending 1st May 1965.

All: *Ray Farrell*

(Right) Britain's first main line diesel electric locomotives No's **10000** (Derby 1947) and **10001** (Derby 1948) head the Up "Royal Scot" between Boars Head and Wigan on 13th June 1959. A 10.00am departure from Glasgow Central coincided with the Down working from Euston which was due to leave at the same time. The "Royal Scot", with no scheduled passenger stops on weekdays was due in Euston at 5.15pm, Saturday's arrival being 80 minutes later at 6.35pm. The Sunday working in contrast had no less than six intermediate calls, prolonging arrival into Euston by a further 1 hour 50 minutes at 8.25pm. The Co-Co's, each rated at 1600hp, were designed and built at Derby, utilising English Electric diesel engined power transmission. The first of the locomotives (10000) was introduced into traffic by the LMS late in 1947. Partner 10001 arrived on the scene after nationalisation in 1948 but their identities were not changed by British Railways. Operated on many occasions as individual units, these forerunners of main line diesel traction are perhaps better remembered as operating in pairs, particularly on the Western lines between London and Scotland although much of the work carried out in the early years was on the Midland main line out of St Pancras, followed by a two year spell on the Southern Region. The view above illustrates the locomotives enjoying what could be described as their 'Indian summer' on one of the country's premier trains although further sightings on the "Royal Scot" were noted later in the month. With the ever increasing introduction of production main line diesels, 10000 and 10001, as 'prototypes', suffered from non-compatibilty with their successors and the inevitable decline in use. 10000 was the first to go, being withdrawn in 1962, whilst 10001 soldiered on for another four years. In retrospect, lives of 15 and 18 years respectively was a good return from the investment, with the pioneering duo in many cases attaining a greater life expectancy than machines they were intended to replace.

Ray Farrell

CHAPTER THREE
WIGAN NORTH WESTERN TO BOARS HEAD JUNCTION

Beyond Wigan No.2 signal box, the route northwards was reduced in capacity to just the Up and Down running lines after crossing the L&Y route to Liverpool/Southport over an acute intersection (Bridge No.44). It continued in this form until Standish Junction where it met and rejoined the Wigan avoiding lines, popularly known as the Whelley Loop, from which point it then ran quadruple all the way to Preston .

The line from Wigan was originally planned as a four line formation and subsequently overbridges at Park Road and Walkden Avenue were designed to facilitate that layout. The opening of the loop bypassing Wigan as early as 1882 and effectively forming an additional pair of lines ensured that the plan never came to fruition.

Rylands Sidings signal box, a 30-lever L.N.W.R. frame stood adjacent to the Up Main line 1 mile 328 yards north of Wigan No.2 and controlled the extensive sidings situated on the westerly or Down side of the running lines. The sidings served as a railhead for several local collieries and also received coal from pits such as Victoria Colliery and Chisnall Hall for screening and washing. Coal operations ceased around 1964 after which the sidings were used for storing permanent way wagons loaded with ballast until final closure. The signal box survived until electrification and was closed 1st October 1972.

From North Western Station the gradient was at 1 in 104 until Boars Head Junction where it eased to 1 in 366 before a final stretch at 1 in 119 to the summit at Coppull Hall Sidings. The Junction was named after the nearby coaching house, which is still going strong.

At the junction, the former Lancashire Union line to Chorley and Blackburn branched off in a north-easterly direction. Opened to goods traffic on 1st November 1869, with passenger traffic following one month later, the line had become little used by the 1960's being regularly traversed only by Wigan–Blackburn parcels and the workers train serving the Royal Ordnance Factory at Euxton, Chorley. Although passenger services were withdrawn 4th January 1960 the route remained open for some time and was utilised for Sunday diversions during upgrade of the now designated West Coast Main Line.

The distinctive Boars Head Junction signal box, an 18-lever LNWR frame, was situated between the Up main line and the Down Adlington Lancashire Union line, 1,463 yards north of Rylands sidings box and was closed 1st October 1972.

Bridge No.53, immediately south of the junction, comprised a central span of 29'-6" and two spans of 26'0" and carried the Wigan-Preston A49 road.

Boars Head station, also situated between the main and branch lines, comprised four platforms serving all four lines and was spanned by an iron footbridge which provided access from the local roads. The station was an early casualty after nationalisation, closing 1st January 1949.

(Right) On 13th June 1959, last Saturday before introduction of the summer timetable, Royal Scot Class '7P' 4-6-0 No **46152** *The Kings Dragoon Guardsman* tackles the 1 in 104 climb from Wigan northwards to Boars Head Junction with the 11.35am ex-London Euston to Whitehaven and Workington Main via Barrow (with Through Carriages (TC) to those destinations, Restaurant Car (RC) service being available between Euston and Crewe. Hardy souls for this nine hour journey were also treated to a buffet service between Preston and Barrow. Allocated to traffic on 20th June 1930 at Crewe North (5A), the 'Scot' was withdrawn from Carlisle Kingmoor (12A) during April 1965.

Ray Farrell

SERVING THE LAKE DISTRICT

(Below) Stanier Princess Coronation Class '8P' 4-6-2 No **46247** *City of Liverpool*, heads the 10.30am ex London Euston to Carlisle train north of Wigan on 28th May 1960. During the week, Restaurant Car facilities were available throughout to Carlisle, but not on Saturdays. Through carriages to Barrow (SO) formed part of the train, the split coming at Lancaster. Through carriages were also included to serve Windermere. The Pacific was built in September 1943 and allocated new to Camden (1B), before moving to its only other base – Carlisle Kingmoor (12A) during June 1961, from where it was withdrawn on 25th May 1963.

Ray Farrell

(Right) Stanier Jubilee No **45678** *De Robeck* of Edge Hill (8A), heads a northbound Class A Excursion train 1X50 past Rylands Sidings towards Boars Head Junction on 20th May 1961. Although the new Four-Position Train Identification system was not due to be in place until the introduction of the Summer Working Time Table commencing 12th June 1961, someone had 'jumped the gun' so to speak. The letter 'X' however was for inter-region trains although the number '50' did not indicate a definite destination *but enabled the use of the same number for outward and return journeys to be maintained.* Rylands Sidings box, a 30 lever LNWR frame, was situated adjacent to the Up line, 1,463 yards south of Boars Head. The box was closed on 1st october 1972. The Jubilee was built in December 1935 and allocated briefly to Crewe North (5A) when new, before moving to Carlisle Upperby (12B) during January 1936. Withdrawal came whilst at Stockport (9B) during December 1962 although at the time of the photograph *De Robeck* was coming towards the end of its tenure at Edge Hill (Liverpool). **Ray Farrell**

(Below) The Blackpool portion of the 10.40 ex-London Euston train clears Rylands Sidings, headed by Crewe North's (5A) Royal Scot Class '7P' 4-6-0 No **46135** *The East Lancashire Regiment* on 13th June 1959. The working shared facilities as far as Crewe with the Holyhead train and was advertised as having Restaurant Car and Through Carriages to Holyhead, with through carriages also to Llandudno, as well as Blackpool Central. Built in 1927, 46135 began its working life at 5A, spending the final four months at Leeds Holbeck (55A) from where it was withdrawn on Christmas Eve 1962. It was a Crewe North engine at the time of this photograph but would shortly be sent to Camden for a very short spell.

Ray Farrell

RYLANDS SIDINGS

(Left) An afternoon stock working had operated between Crewe and Carlisle at various times over the years. On Saturday 10th April 1965 this unidentified 'Brittania' 4-6-2 locomotive (less nameplates) climbs towards Rylands Sidings signal box, the home signal on this right-hand bracket raised to give a clear road ahead. The small arm on the lower 'doll' is for entry into the sidings situated nearer the signal box which was located on the Up side. The train was timed passing Rylands at 15.40 with headlamp code which suggests possibly an empty coaching-stock train. As steam traction slowly ground to its ultimate demise, the majority of the class found their way to Carlisle (Kingmoor) for withdrawal prior to storage. *E F Bentley*

(Below) Stanier Class '5' 4-6-0 No **45276** tackles the final stages of the 1 in 104 to Boars Head Junction with a Uttoxeter to Blackpool excursion train (1Z30) on 5th October 1963. The letter 'Z' indicated that the train was a local working between Districts within the London Midland Region, i.e; Stoke, Blackpool and Fylde. The Class '5' was introduced to traffic at Gloucester (22B) on 14th November 1936 and had moved several times before arriving at Stoke (5D) during August 1963, and was withdrawn from the Potteries depot during January 1967. *Ray Farrell*

(Right) 'WD' Austerity Class '8F' 2-8-0 No **90375** climbs past Rylands Sidings towards Boars Head Junction with a northbound freight on 5th October 1963 carrying headlamp code for a Class 6 'Through Fast Train'. Built in February 1946, the '8F' was at this time based at Lower Darwen (24D-10H) and was withdrawn from there during July 1964.

(Centre) Although British Railways steam still had seventeen months active service at the time of this photograph, Gresley 'A4' 4-6-2 No **4498** *Sir Nigel Gresley* had already been purchased privately in May 1966 following a desire to preserve an A4 in operating condition. 4498 however, was in a run-down condition and subsequently an overhaul commenced in August 1966 at Crewe, restoring it to its LNER identity. On 5th March 1967, the A4 Locomotive Society formally came into being and this was followed on 1st April by a rail tour from Crewe to Carlisle via Shap, returning via the Settle & Carlisle. Amongst its running in turns were the 23.45 Crewe to Preston parcels 3P07 and the 05.30 Preston to Crewe local passenger, 2K82. The Pacific makes light work of the climb away from Wigan on the outward journey of its 1st April tour. The locomotive is now operated and maintained by the Sir Nigel Gresley Locomotive Preservation Trust Ltd.

(Below) Royal Scot Class '7P' 4-6-0 No **46123** *Royal Irish Fusilier* drifts downhill from Boars Head Junction towards Wigan with a southbound passenger train, the 2.30am ex-Morecambe Promenade to Crewe on 28th May 1960. Built in 1927 and allocated to Crewe North (5A), 46123 was an early victim to the cutters torch, being withdrawn from Upperby (12B) on 31st October 1962. However, it remains something of a mystery how a Kentish Town (14B) based loco finds itself near Wigan in May 1960.   All; *Ray Farrell*

(Left) A Glasgow-Birmingham express headed by Stanier Princess Coronation Class '8P' 4-6-2 No **46221** *Queen Elizabeth*, starts the descent southwards from Boars Head towards Wigan on 23rd May 1959. The elevated signal box at Boars Head is visible above the rear coach of the train, through the centre arch of the road bridge. Carrying Wigan Road towards Chorley, bridge No 53 comprised a central arch of 29'-6" spanning the dual track, with supporting arches of 26'-0" span at each side. Built in June 1937, the Stanier Pacific spent just over two years at Camden (1B) and Crewe North (5A), before moving permanently north to Polmadie (66B) on Christmas Eve 1939, where it was to remain until July 1958 when it returned to Crewe. Withdrawal from Upperby (12B) came on 17th May 1963. *Ray Farrell*

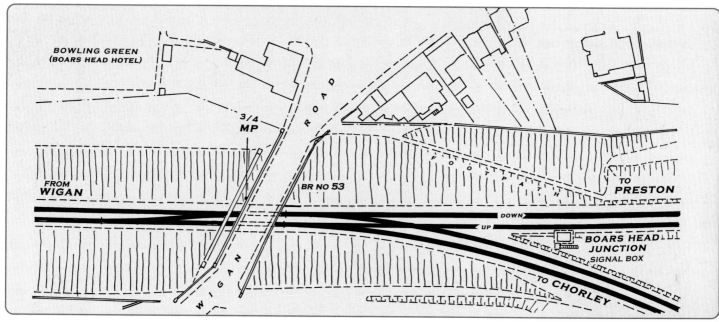

BOARS HEAD
JUNCTION

(Right) British Railways Class '7P6F' 4-6-2 No **70000** *Britannia* heads a train for Blackpool, approaching the top of the climb from Wigan to Boars Head on 5th October 1963. The first of the successful BR Pacifics, No 70000 was built in January 1951 and allocated to Stratford (30A) where it stayed until January 1959. The engine moved to Newton Heath (26A-9D) on 2nd April 1966 and was withdrawn before the end of May. The name *Britannia* was originally carried by Jubilee Class 4-6-0 No 45700, before being transferred to the eponymous BR 4-6-2, the Jubilee being re-named *Amethyst*. *Ray Farrell*

An Upperby (12B) Jubilee Class No **45599** *Bechuanaland* begins the descent towards Wigan, passing Boars Head Junction signal box with a southbound express on 13th June 1959. Two days later, the Jubilee, built in January 1935 and allocated new to Derby (17A-16C) moved to Camden (1B) and was finally withdrawn from Nuneaton (2B-5E) during August 1964. The distinctive signal box, an 18 lever LNW frame, was situated between the Up Main line and the Down ex-Lancashire Union line to Chorley via Red Rock and the quaintly named White Bear. Passenger services between Chorley (Adlington Jcn) and Wigan via Boars Head were withdrawn on 4th January 1960 and completely to all traffic by the end of December 1971. The signal box was closed on 1st October 1972.   *Ray Farrell*

Stanier Princess Coronation Class No **46240** *City of Coventry* passing Boars Head Junction with a London Euston –Windermere train on 13th June 1959. The former Lancashire Union railway to Red Rock and Chorley is seen diverging to the left. The Pacific, built on 27th March 1940, spent all but one of its 24 year life span at Camden (1B) where it was based at this time. After moving via Willesden (1A) to Crewe North (5A), its original base when new, 46240 was withdrawn during week ending 12th September 1964.

Ray Farrell

(Right) Unrebuilt Patriot Class '6P5F' 4-6-0 No **45538** *Giggleswick* heads south past Boars Head Junction with W254, 10.50am ex-Workington and Whitehaven via Barrow to London Euston on 13th June 1959. For those with culinary interests, a Buffet Car was provided between Workington and Preston and Restaurant Car between Preston and London Euston, no doubt to the delight of Workington folk who had already been on the train for almost four hours. At the time a Preston loco (24K), the Patriot was built in January 1935 and allocated briefly to Derby (17A-16C), before lengthy spells at Holbeck (55A) – 12 years, and Edge Hill (8A) – 8 years. Withdrawn on 20th September 1962, the loco spent its last active 8 months at Nuneaton (2B-5E). ***Ray Farrell***

(Below) Stanier Class '5' 4-6-0 No **45122** heads an Up freight past the elevated signal box at Boars Head Junction on 5th October 1963. Originally having four platforms, only the graded section around the signal box now remains. 45122 was introduced to traffic at Crewe North (5A) on 29th June 1935. Lengthy spells at Inverness (60A) where the loco spent 11 years, and Kingmoor (12A) 11½ years, preceded withdrawal from the Carlisle depot during April 1964. ***Ray Farrell***

(Left) Speke Junction (8C) provides the motive power for this Halewood – Bathgate Ford car train, as Stanier Class '5' 4-6-0 No **45071** powers past Boars Head Junction signal box, having just topped the 1 in 104 climb from Wigan in fine style on 27th June 1964. It had been normal to route the train via the Whelley Loop so the event here cannot be explained. Introduced to traffic when new in May 1935 at Crewe North (5A), the Class '5' had moved to Speke during October 1961 and was withdrawn from there on 20th July 1967. It is this view more than most which illustrates the need for the somewhat elevated position of the box which was required to facilitate the one-time station platforms and buildings immediately below.

(Below) Jubilee Class '6P5F' 4-6-0 No **45661** *Vernon* of Newton Heath (26A-9D) heads a Crewe – Blackpool train past Boars Head Junction on 27th June 1964. Built in December 1934, the Jubilee spent some 25 years at the Manchester motive power depot, the remaining time being spent in various forays across the Pennines to Holbeck (55A) Farnley Junction (55C) and Wakefield (56A). Withdrawal came on 17th May 1965 from Holbeck where the locomotive began its 'career' back in December 1934.   Both: *Ray Farrell*

In a picturesque setting not normally associated with Wigan, the Down "Mid-day Scot", with Princess Coronation Class 4-6-2 No **46255** *City of Hereford* at the head, passes Boars Head Junction (approx 5.23pm - 3minutes was allowed in the section for recovery time if late) on 28th May 1960. Departing Euston at 1.05pm the train was due in Glasgow at 8.20pm. 46255 was a post war built member of the class, allocated new to Camden in October 1946. Withdrawn from Kingmoor (12A) during September 1964, the Pacific was based at Upperby (12B) at the time of this photograph.

Ray Farrell

The Up "Mid-day Scot" passes Boars Head Junction (approx 5.37pm) with Princess Coronation Class No **46237** *City of Bristol* in charge on 28th May 1960. Seen curving away to the right above the engine tender is the former Lancashire Union line to Chorley via Red Rock. With a scheduled departure at 1.15 pm from Glasgow Central, the "Mid-days" would pass south of Leyland, the Up train being due in Euston at 8.30 pm. Built in August 1939, the Pacific spent brief spells at Camden (1B), Longsight (9A) and Rugby (2A-1F), before returning to Camden for a 13 year spell, broken only by a three week loan period to Upperby (12B) in May 1952. Finding its way north to Carlisle, *City of Bristol* was withdrawn from Upperby (12B) during September 1964.
Ray Farrell

Organised by the Railway Travel & Correspondence Society to give what 'may well be the last opportunity to travel from Crewe to Edinburgh (Princes Street) behind a Duchess', this special, headed by No **46251** *City of Nottingham* finds some relief from the change in gradient as it passes Boars Head Junction during the early stages of the outward journey. It had originally been intended to use No 46256 *Sir William A Stanier* but the discovery of a defect on the front bogie of the loco the previous week resulted in the replacement. An eleven coach train of LMS stock, including M8950M from the "Coronation Scot" was provided for the tour which attracted some 350 participants as well as the lineside throngs. A start from Crewe at 8.57am saw 46251 reach Warrington Bank Quay at 9.24, twenty seven minutes for the 24 miles. The journey north did not continue particularly quickly, Wigan being passed at 9.41am. From Boars Head however, the long straight and slightly falling stretch to Leyland enabled *City of Nottingham* to attain 74mph before a permanent way check at the latter halted the train's progress. Arrival in Preston was at 9.59am. The remainder of the journey falls outside the scope of this book although the outward working is covered by noting passing times at some of the relative locations. Lancaster was passed at 10.34am, Carnforth at 10.40am where a speed of 79mph was noted, follwed by Oxenholme (10.51am), Grayrigg (11.3am) and Tebay (11.10am) where time was taken for Fowler 2-6-4T No 42414 to buffer up for the climb to Shap. Racing down to Penrith (pass 11.35) saw 46251 attain 76mph, before reaching the highest speed on the northbound near Plumpton where 80/84mph was recorded. Arrival in Carlisle was at 11.53am, where engines took place for the remainder of the run to Edinburgh (arr 2.8pm).

Ray Farrell

(**Left**) The second of our two photographs of the northbound leg of the "Duchess" Commemorative Rail Tour shows No **46251** *City of Nottingham* passing Boars Head Junction on Saturday 5th October 1963. Called upon at the last minute as a replacement, 46251 was resplendent from all angles and put in a splendid performance considering the declining maintenance standards as Britain's railways moved towards the end of main line steam. The return journey would see the train pass Boars Head Junction about 7.40pm in the evening, enabling completion of the tour at Crewe at 8.28, only three minutes late. Built in June 1944, the Stanier Pacific, after a brief initial spell at Camden (1B), moved north to Polmadie (66A) and was finally withdrawn from Crewe North (5A) during September 1964.

Ray Farrell

(Left) A southbound fitted freight headed by Stanier Class '5' 4-6-0 No **45371** of Carlisle Upperby (12B) drifts downgrade past Boars Head Junction on the descent towards Wigan on 5th October 1963. The engine spent its early years in North Wales being introduced to traffic at Llandudno Junction (6G) on 14th June 1937 and returning there for a four year stay after a brief visit to Holyhead (6J). Moving north due to re-allocation the loco was withdrawn after a brief stay at Workington (11B-12D) during April 1967. *Ray Farrell*

(Centre) LMS built 4F 0-6-0 No **44081** heads south near Boars Head Junction with 3F66, a Blackpool North – Wigan Springs Branch empty carriage working on 27th June 1964. This train, consisting of compartment stock, had left Blackpool North at 12 noon following an outward day excursion from St Helens Shaw Street to the seaside resort and was due to cover Saturdays 20th and 27th only. The presence of an Upperby (12B) engine carrying out such duties was consistent with the demands of holiday traffic when almost any type of engine was called upon to help out. The '4F' had been a Carlisle Upperby (12B) engine for many years and it was from there that that 44081 was withdrawn during September 1965. *Ray Farrell*

(Left) Stanier 2–cylinder class '4' 2-6-4t No **42607**, based locally at Springs Branch (8F), heads past Boars Head Junction with the 9.30am Wigan North Western – Preston local on 5th October 1963. It is surprising that this local service lasted as long as it did, keeping Coppull and Balshaw Lane & Euxton on the national network until 6th October 1969. On Saturdays there were seven northbound trains but with a gap of five hours after 9.30am, it was difficult to see any benefit. The three coach formation was the norm. The engine, built in December 1936 and initially allocated to Stockport (9B), the 2-6-4T was withdrawn from its Wigan base just four months later at the end of January 1964. *Ray Farrell*

(Above) Following a very interesting discussion with the Boars Head Junction signalman on 20th July 1963, it was pointed out that the train seen here, hauled by rebuilt Patriot Class '7P' 4-6-0 No **45545** *Planet,* was in fact a Folkestone to Edinburgh troop special. Workings such as this would be notified to the appropriate staff through the Weekly Notices, or SDN's as they were popularly known. They were a regular feature when mass movement of the military were carried out. Built in March 1934, *Planet* was allocated to Kentish Town (14B) when new. Despite its excellent external condition, reflecting credit on its Upperby (12B) domicile, the Patriot was withdrawn from its Carlisle base just 10 months later at the end of May 1964.
Ray Farrell

Right) This time on 5th October 1963 at Boars Head with rebuilt No **45545** *Planet,* still in pristine external condition, heading a Class 4 express freight towards Wigan. *Ray Farrell*

(Right) In sparkling sunlight, a Warrington Dallam (8B) locomotive, Stanier Class '5' 4-6-0 No **45414**, nears Boars Head Junction with southbound express freight on 5th October 1963. As the majority of unfitted or partially fitted freights were still routed via the Whelley loop south of Standish, trains such as this were relatively infrequent on the two line section to Wigan North Western. This locomotive, introduced to traffic on 28th September 1937, had moved via Speke Junction (8C) to Carlisle Upperby (12B) in January 1938 and was to spend twenty-two years there before moving on. 45414 was withdrawn from Edge Hill (8A) by early February 1965.
Ray Farrell

(Centre) Clearing the 1 in 104 climb northwards from Wigan to Boars Head Junction, Upperby (12B) Stanier 'Jubilee' 4-6-0 No **45737** *Atlas*, is at the head of a London Euston to Glasgow train on 30th July 1960. Allocated to Crewe North (5A) when new in November 1936, the Jubilee found its way to Newton Heath (26A-9D) during March 1962 and was withdrawn from the Manchester depot during June 1964.
Ray Farrell

(Below) Stanier Jubilee Class '6P5F' 4-6-0 No **45726** *Vindictive* heads a southbound parcels train near Boars Head Junction on 20th June 1964. Built in December 1936, the Jubilee spent its early years on the eastern side of the Pennines, moving from Low Moor (56F) to Farnley Junction (55C) and then to Leeds Holbeck (55A). In June 1942 the loco was re-allocated, this time to Lancashire with a move to Edge Hill (8A) and was withdrawn whilst at Warrington Dallam (8B) during March 1965 having moved there in December 1963.
Ray Farrell

Another Stanier 'Jubilee', this time No **45696** *Arethusa,* heads a southbound freight on the Up Fast line past Standish Junction signal box on a dismal Lancashire day, 27th June 1964. This much travelled engine, which was built in April 1936 and allocated new to Newton Heath (26A-9D), had eventually arrived at Carlisle Kingmoor (12A) in June 1963 and after withdrawal in July of the following year was cut up at J.W.Connell of Coatbridge. The signal box, with a 72 lever LNWR tumbler frame, located in the centre of the quadrupled track layout at the northern end of the one time four platformed station, was closed 21st October 1972.

Ray Farrell

Continuing on from Boars Head, Standish Junction lay 1m. 6ch further north with Victoria Colliery and associated sidings the only significant feature in the short double line stretch. Victoria Colliery Sidings signal box was situated 724 yds north of Boars Head adjacent to the Up line controlling the colliery sidings on the west side of the line. It was closed on 20th September 1964.

At Standish Junction the loop lines joined, the Down Whelley passing under the main line (see photo on page 62) and the Up loop forking away in a south-easterly direction beyond the bridge (No 62) at a point where the Euston to Glasgow line came together as the Up and Down Main to Wigan. The route to Euxton was quadrupled in 1895.

On summer Saturdays, numerous excursion trains arrived onto the main line at Standish via the Whelley line, some having travelled via the former Great Central route from Glazebrook. The only booked passenger working on this route was the 17.10pm Manchester Exchange-Windermere.

Considerable freight used the Whelley line but this was much reduced by the mid 1960's and southbound drivers would often decline the route claiming they were not passed on it to avoid the delays a diversion onto the Whelley would cause. The loop survived until electrification of the main line being closed on 2nd October 1972.

Standish station, situated between the junctions, with access from Rectory Lane, was known as Standish Lane until 1844 and was closed in May 1949.

Coppull Hall Sidings signal box, situated 1m 734 yds north of Standish was a 30-lever LNWR frame which stood adjacent to the Down Slow line just north of the sidings it controlled and was another early casualty being closed on 17th December 1969.

A further 1,423 yds north was Blainscough Sidings box, a 40-lever LNWR tumbler frame, this one located next to the Up Fast and controlling the main lines as well as the sidings situated on the west of the running lines, was closed on 5th November 1972. Coppull Station platforms, which served the slow lines only, was immediately north of the Blainscough box and was closed on 6th October 1969.

Yet another siding to service the coal industry was at Darlingtons Sidings, approximately $1/2$ mile north of Coppull, the signal box of that name being closed on 20th September 1964.

Further north the Up and Down lines separated for a distance before converging just beyond Balshaw Lane and Euxton Station situated 2 m 117 yds beyond Darlingtons Sidings and like its near neighbour Coppull, served only the slow lines. The 25-lever tumbler frame LNWR box situated between the Up Fast and Down Slow just south of the platforms closed on 5th November 1972. A new station was opened on the site of the old in 1997.

(Right) Burton (17B-16F) based Stanier Jubilee 4-6-0 No **45721** *Impregnable* heads 1M06, the 8.25am Leicester London Road – Blackpool North, on the single line northbound spur of the Whelley loop on 27th June 1964. This summer special ran on the last Saturday in June and Saturdays throughout July and August. It followed a route which nowadays would have the enthusiast drooling by its itinerary. First stop out of Leicester was Loughborough before picking up at Trent and traversing the Erewash Valley for Chesterfield. The Dore and Chinley route was accessed at Dore West Junction, enabling the Derby to Manchester line to be joined at Chinley. On occasion, an engine and/or crew change could take place at Cheadle Heath, time being allowed for water if necessary. Somewhat 'foreign' territory was then encountered as the train headed for Skelton Junction and Glazebrook before taking the Wigan line as far as Amberswood East Junction. The Whelley loop was now encountered, enabling the avoidance of Wigan and thus joining the Euston-Glasgow route at

Standish Junction after passing beneath the main line (Br No 61), taking the Slow line as far as Preston. There was something of a long standing tradition about these summer Saturdays Only East Midlands to the Fylde trains but it was all coming to an end, cemented into history with the closure of Blackpool Central in November 1964. Built in August 1936, the Jubilee was initially allocated to Blackpool (24E-10B) when new and followed a nomadic journey around the LMS and BR. Its stay at Burton was short lived and a transfer to Bank Hall in October 1964 followed from where it was ultimately withdrawn in October 1965.

(Centre) Not a train in sight but the crew of special 1M06 (seen above) would recognise the bridge (North Union No 61) as the point where the Down Whelley was about to join the west coast main line at Standish Junction. To achieve this however, there was a short sharp stretch at 1 in 74 which required that one last ounce of effort to leave the avoiding line behind. This view of the western elevation (Down side) of the bridge, taken on 16th April 1959, shows the structure carrying the main line with Preston to the left and Wigan to the right. The SO special (1M06) seen above, was the last of the northbound workings to use the link on the day. The others would be 1M02 Sheffield Midland-Blackpool Central; 1P26 (Desford to Blackpool North); 1P35 (Manchester Vic-Blackpool North); 1M03 (Nottingham Midland-Blackpool North); 1M04 Chesterfield Central-Blackpool North); 1M05 (Cleethorpes-Blackpool North).

(right) Stanier class '5' 4-6-0 No **44966** of Aston (3D-2J) heads 1P42 the 9.35am Birmingham (New Street) – Blackpool (North) through Standish Junction on 27th June 1964. The view is looking south from the signal box steps with the train travelling north on the Down line from Wigan and approaching a point from where the route quadruples, the Down line becoming the Down Fast (whilst crossing over) and the Down Whelley Loop, having passed under the main line, emerging to become the Down Slow on the right of the locomotive (i.e. west side).The letter 'P' of the reporting number indicates the destination district which in this instance is Blackpool and Fylde. Built in August 1946 and allocated new to Nottingham (16A-16D) the Class '5' had by this time arrived at Aston during April 1964 and was withdrawn from Shrewsbury (84G) by late September 1966 for cutting at Cashmore –Great Bridge.   All: ***Ray Farrell***

(Right) A pair of Crewe North (5A) Stanier locomotives, leading engine Class '5' 4-6-0 No **44759** and 'Jubilee' 4-6-0 No **45556** *Nova Scotia*, double head W156, the 10.15am Edinburgh – Birmingham away from Standish Junction on 30th July 1960. The descent to Wigan commences at 1 in 366 from Standish followed by the now well documented 1 in 104 as far as North Western station. Built in September 1947 and allocated to Perth (63A), the Class '5' survived until November 1967 when withdrawn from Kingmoor (12A). *Nova Scotia,* built some 13 years earlier in June 1934, ended its days at Crewe North (5A) and was withdrawn by early September 1964.

(Centre) This picture is included to illustrate that British Railways, whilst in the process of developing its motive power requirements, made resources available for other projects such as the intersection bridge (No 61) south of Standish which enabled the Down Whelley line (for northbound trains) to pass beneath the main line and join it at Standish junction. This view, taken on 3rd September 1963, shows the view north towards Standish (and Preston) after the bridge had been reconstructed. The wrought iron girders seen opposite have been replaced by a brick and concrete structure. The line opposite at lower level which disappears beneath the bridge is visible in the picture here to the left of the new parapet at a lower level. Although not totally clear, the pictures at the top and bottom of this page are in the vicinity of this intersection bridge but give a clear indication of the converging of the lines after passing either side of the site of Standish station's central island platform.

(Right) Having passed the site of the long closed Standish station, the Up and Down main lines come together beyond Rectory Lane bridge - note parapets to the extreme left - for the 12.20pm Preston to Wigan North Western local, headed by Stanier 2-cylinder Class '4' 2-6-4 tank No **42601**, on 27th June 1964. Some twenty years earlier, as WW2 was entering its final stages, the 12.20pm (12.25 on Saturdays) was operating and due to call at Standish (arr 12.48) and Boars Head (arr 12.53). Despite the closures of these stations, the 12.20 continued

to run until withdrawal of the service in 1969. Built in November 1936, the Class '4' was allocated to Rugby (2A-1F) before moving to Barrow (11A-2C) and then on to Carnforth (24L-10A) in July 1940 where, apart from two weeks on loan to Aston (3D-2J), it was to stay until March 1955. The locomotive was based at Springs Branch (8F) at the time of this photograph and was withdrawn from there by early April 1965.   All: *Ray Farrell*

(Right) A view looking south from the overgrown platform that was Standish station on 27th June 1964. Stanier Class '5' 4-6-0's No **44673** and **44816**, both of Lostock Hall (24C-10D) double-head a Down train bound for Whitehaven. Note the signals to the left, the extreme left arm (Lever No 9) which controlled movements on to the Up Whelley Line whilst the lower arm on the bracket (Lever 4) was for the Up Main to Wigan and beyond. The partially smoke concealed signal was the former platform signal for Up movements, again for the Wigan line. Built in November 1944 and allocated new to Kentish Town, 44816 returned to Lostock on 1st October 1967 and was withdrawn from the Lancashire depot during week ending 20th July 1968, just two weeks before the end of steam on British Rail. 44673, introduced to traffic during February 1950 at Carlisle Kingmoor (12A) was not so fortunate, moving to Trafford Park (9E) in February 1965 and being withdrawn from the Manchester depot during May of that year. *Ray Farrell*

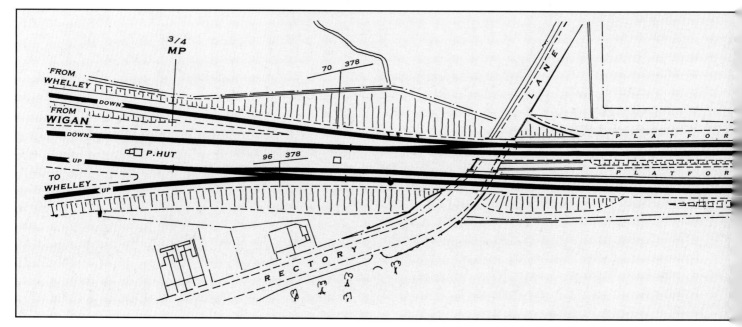

(Right) The decline in steam haulage on the main lines had been gathering pace as quickly as British Railways had been in adopting a standardisation process for its diesel fleets. Having seen the early prototypes come and go, the Brush Type '4' had now well and truly entrenched itself on the LM route to Scotland. Here at Standish Junction on 24th September 1966 (Saturday), **D1860** heads northbound with 1S75, a London Euston to Glasgow train, the loco beginning the transfer from the Down Main to the Down Fast on the quadrupled section to Euxton Junction. The turnout in the foreground enabled trains off the Down Whelley line to be routed on to the Down Slow or Down Fast. Although there is little trace to be seen in this picture the platform of the erstwhile Standish station began at a point just beyond the right hand signal. D1860 became 47 210 following T.O.P.S renumbering, having originally emerged from BR Crewe in September 1965. *Graham Whitehead*

(Right) A southbound 'mixed' freight headed by a Carlisle Kingmoor (12A) British Railways Standard Class '7P6F' 4-6-2 No **70039** *Sir Christopher Wren* passes Standish Junction signal box - and the site of the station closed 23rd May 1949, a few months ahead of Boars Head - on 27th June 1964. Built in February 1953 and allocated new to Norwich (32A), 70039 moved to Kingmoor in February 1964, withdrawal from service coming in September 1967 whilst at the Carlisle depot. The 'Britannia' was dispatched to J.McWilliam, Shettleston for cutting up on 25th January 1968. Reverting to the station itself, Standish spent its life appearing on the pages of the main line timetables. It was as well placed to serve the village it took its

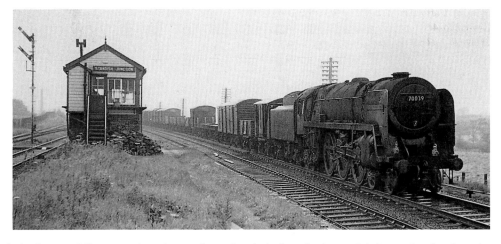

name from but unfortunately could never attract the business to fully support its existence, hence its relatively early closure. It is interesting that throughout WW2 there were seven northbound trains calling and nine heading south, all basically part of a Preston/Wigan local service although a small number contrived to start or finish at Warrington. Scheduled basically to a 'peak' period pattern, covering morning and late afternoon, with nothing in the middle of the day save for a mid-day southbound SO train, this situation continued until closure. The irony of this is that the basic Preston/Wigan service, containing a similar number of trains, survived until 1969.

Ray Farrell

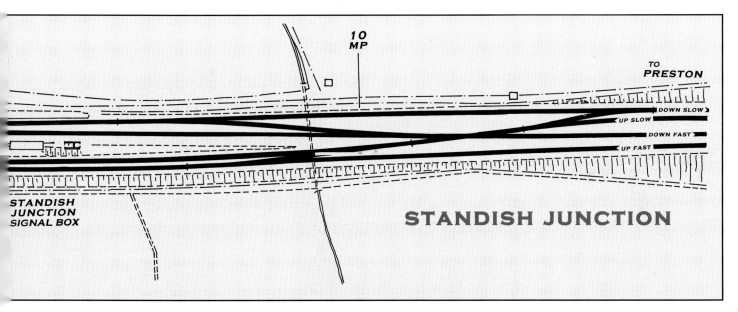

STANDISH JUNCTION
SIGNAL BOX

STANDISH JUNCTION

10 MP

TO PRESTON

DOWN SLOW
UP SLOW
DOWN FAST
UP FAST

(Left) This London Euston bound train 1M35, from Glasgow Central, has just cleared the Standish Junction outer home signal which clears the route for Brush Type '4' No **D1841** to proceed along the Up main towards Wigan North Western. Some of the type '4' diesels were restricted when it came to the maximum tonnage which was to be conveyed by the locomotive. In the case of a small number of Anglo-Scottish trains, a code in the Working Timetable contained the letter 'D' with three figures that followed. The 'Scottish ' trains were designated D420 which indicated the maximum tonnage. The view here also shows the configuration of the layout north of Standish Junction and how it segregated the four lines into two separate routes, the main line to Wigan and the Whelley loop which of course avoided the town. D1841 became 47191 in the T.O.P.S renumbering.

Graham Whitehead

(Right) Carlisle Kingmoor (12A) Stanier Class '5' 4-6-0 No **44668** heads a northbound freight on the Down Slow near Standish Junction on 30th July 1960. Introduced to traffic at Kingmoor on 23rd December 1949, the Class '5' had no other recorded motive power depots and was withdrawn from its Carlisle base during April 1966. *Ray Farrell*

(Centre) A Kentish Town (14B) Jubilee, Class '6P5F' 4-6-0 No **45561** *Saskatchewan* heads south near Standish Junction with W268, the 3.40pm ex-Blackpool North to Walsall, on 30th July 1960. Built in July 1934, the Jubilee was initially allocated to Camden (1B) but spent just one week there moving to Crewe North (5A) and then on to Preston (24K). At the time of withdrawal during september 1964, the Jubilee was resident at Derby (17A-16C) *Ray Farrell*

Positioned in the Down Slow 'four-foot' looking south towards Standish Junction, the photographer takes the precaution of facing any oncoming traffic which there is in the distance. This view, taken on 1st August 1963 shows the quadrupled section of the 'North Union' immediately north of Coppull Ha Sidings signal box, the structure itself being just visible behind the right hand pier of the occupation bridge (No 69). Although not absolutely clear, Standis Junction distant signals can just be seen above the bridge in the distance. The signal box also marks the end of a five mile climb from Wigan. *BR(LMR*

(Above) Standing between the headshunt of Coppull goods yard and the Down Slow line, we look south in the direction of Wigan with footbridge (No 72) across the foreground. Coppull Parish Church is to the left of the picture. It is somewhat difficult to imagine the tree-less panorama of 25th July 1963 over four decades on. Only the pair of running lines to the left of the picture are in operation today, Virgin Trains *Pendolinos* rushing by, no doubt behind a curtain of lineside vegetation, obscuring the view from Chapel Lane.

A twenty coach train was is an impressive sight no matter what the motive power is. On this occasion, Class 5MT 4-6-0 No **45039** heads south on the Up Fast line towards Wigan with 3T32, an ECS (Empty Coaching Stock) working on 13th June 1965. The photographer has managed this carriage window view from a train on the Up Slow line having just left Coppull, the station buildings which appear in the centre left of the picture. The roof outline above the second carriage of the ECS belongs to the Railway Hotel, located alongside the course of the old road that existed before quadrupling of the line between Standish junction and Euxton Junction. The loco had been a loyal servant to Edge Hill (Liverpool-8A) since August 1951 and it was from that depot from which it was withdrawn in August 1967.

N K Harrop

67

(Left) Coppull on a winter's day, 3rd December 1964. Dr Beeching's cull of the railways had not yet reached Coppull and judging by the fixtures, fittings and other items on the platform, the station had other ideas, for four years at least. A northbound stopping train leaves for Preston in this view north. *G Biddle*

SOUTH ROAD

ESCENT

LOADING

FROM WIGAN

5 TON CRANE

W. COL

DOWN SLOW   UP SLOW

DOWN FAST   UP FAST

BLAINSCOUGH SIDINGS SIG. BOX

RAILWAY

(Above) Coppull, 25th July 1959. A unique rail level view of the 'North Union'; lines south of Coppull station. The photographer is standing in the Up Slow 'four-foot' pointing his camera in a northerly direction towards Euxton Junction and Preston. Coppull station's two platforms are located either side of the slow lines, where a slight deviation was required to accommodate the station. Signalling at this location came under the control of Blainscough Sidings box, seen here to the right of the picture alongside the Up Fast. The box was an LNWR type 4 structure with a 40 lever tumbler frame. Closure of the box took place on 5th November 1972. Goods facilities were withdrawn on 6th October 1969 but some sidings remained in use under private ownership. Passenger services were also withdrawn on 6th October 1969. The footbridge (No 72) was a typical design that superceded the well known pattern containing cast-iron colums and balusters. It was consistent with the other similar structures along the North Union.

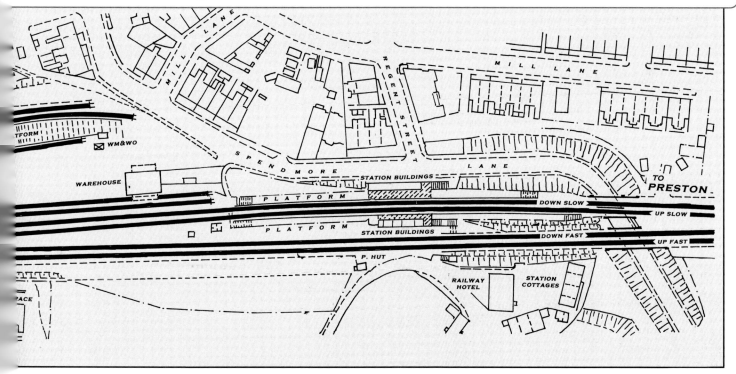

The station, goods yard and associated sidings at Coppull extended for over a mile of the fifteen or so between Wigan and Preston. Coppull station itself came under the control of Blainscough Sidings signal box, the irony of this being that the colliery of that name was accessed immediately to the south of the signal box seen above which was called Darlingtons Sidings after the name of the family who were owners in the area of several deep mine shaft collieries. The photographer is positioned in the 'four-foot' of the Down Fast line, looking south in the direction of Wigan, in the views on these pages taken on 25th July 1963. All the signals are shown in the 'off' position suggesting that the box is 'switched

out'. Although acting as a block post for trains on the fast lines, there were no Fast/Slow crossover facilities between Standish Junction and Euxton Junction. A reduction in use of the Slow lines by this time enabled Darlingtons Sidings box to become redundant, being closed from 20th September 1964, some fourteen months after this picture was taken and one of the earlier rationalisation statistics in the signalling department. Behind the signal box is the Coppull Ring Mill of the Lancashire Cotton Corporation Ltd., a mill built in 1906. We have no knowledge of when spinning was curtailed but the building, with its very distinctive dome, was converted in the 1980's by Lancashire

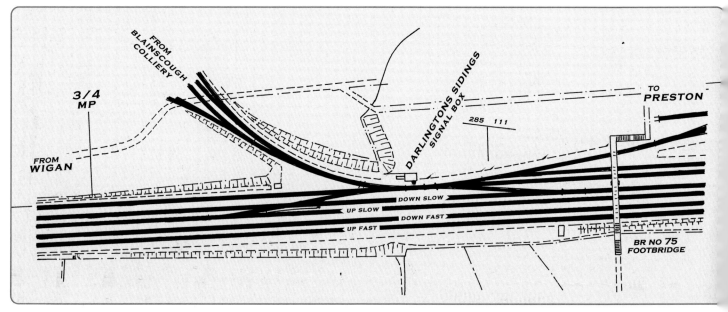

Enterprises to become the Coppull Enterprise Centre and provides something of a landmark in the area these days. The large mill the right is Mavis Mill, built in 1908 and combined with its neighbour, employed between 700 and 1000 people at its peak. Mavis Mill is believed to have been demolished in the 1970's. The connection to Blainscough Colliery was still in place at the time of the photograph although the pit, opened in 1879, had ceased coal production in 1939. Coppull station platforms are located less than half a mile away in the distance either side of the Slow lines, the third and fourth (left to right) running lines in the above picture. Nowadays, the fast lines (to the left) are all that remain of this con-

centration of railway infrastructure although quadrupling does recommence again a short distance beyond the 14 milepost at what is now Balshaw Lane Junction.

(Below) Taking up a position in the Up Slow line, the cameraman now looks in a northerly direction towards Euxton Junction and subsequently Preston. The Fast lines are to the right whilst the sidings (to the left), formerly serving Blainscough Colliery, await their fate. Surprisingly, the colliery siding connection with the main line did not materialise until 1899. Two youngsters take time to view the proceedings from the footbridge (No 75).

BALSHAW LANE & EUXTON

Balshaw Lane & Euxton, to give its full title, was located just under three quarters of a mile south of the first Euxton station as a result of the 1895 quadrupling. The station buildings, on the original North Union alignment which became the 'Slow' lines, were of 'standard' LNWR sectional wooden buildings. Accessed from Balshaw Lane, the station lost its passenger services on 6th October 1969. Goods facilities had been withdrawn on 8th March 1965. The view here shows an Up local passenger train c.1965 when Stanier Class 4 2-6-4T No **42287** was for a short spell based at Lostock Hall shed. ***Authors collection***

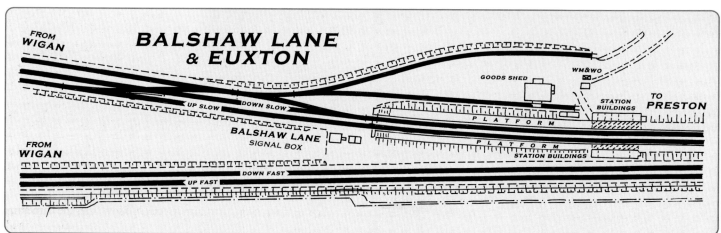

An Edge Hill (8A) Jubilee Class 4-6-0 No **45586** *Mysore* heads a southbound express between Euxton Junction and Balshaw Lane on 11th April 1959. Considering the early tender transfer, the loco appears to be in remarkable external condition for 1959, which is when it was fitted with automatic train alarm gear. The leading 'porthole' brake third was built br BR to LMS diagram D2161 whilst D1807 Period 2 open third, three Stanier corridor thirds, another D1807 open third and a further Stanier brake third are genuine LMS coaches. The much travelled Jubilee lost its 4000 gallon tender to 'Royal Scot' No 6148 and recieved a 3500 gallon tender in exchange. *Mysore* is recorded as having 32 moves during its 30 year life, starting at Crewe North (5A) in December 1934 and terminating on withdrawal from Crewe South (5B) during 1965. The Slow lines are across the lower left of the picture. ***Ray Farrell***

Stanier Princess Coronation Class '8P' 4-6-2 No **46234** *Duchess of Abercorn* heads a Birmingham to Glasgow train along the Down Fast between Coppull and Balshaw Lane & Euxton on 11th April 1959. From Wigan northwards to Standish there were only two running lines, the Up and the Down. It was quadrupled from Standish Junction onwards to accommodate traffic to and from the Whelley Loop, Slow lines, including the stations at Coppull and Balshaw Lane. These were to the west side which catered for local services and goods traffic. The Fast lines, without any stations or connections with the Slow lines, were located on the east side, hence the view of the train here on its northbound journey. The Pacific, which started life at Camden (1B), had moved on to Crewe North (5A) at this time and was withdrawn from Carlisle Upperby (12B) on 23rd January 1963. *Ray Farrell*

Patriot Class '6P5F' 4-6-0 No **45537** *Private E. Sykes* V.C. (12B - Upperby) heads a lengthy southbound freight, the 6.50 ex- Carlisle to Crewe Gresty Green, between Euxton Junction and Balshaw Lane on 11th April 1959. The engine is about to pass over School Lane bridge (No 89), constructed as a result of the 1895 quadrupling which eliminated the level crossing at this point. The buildings to the right of the 'Patriot' follow the old road. The footbridge (No 90) replaced a footpath at that location and careful scrutiny at the base of the structure reveals a $1/2$ milepost ($15^{1}/_{2}$ from Parkside). The 'Patriot' Class were generally acknowledged as good engines by footplate crews and would be at ease with a train of this type, performing quite comfortably at 45 to 50mph. Built in July 1933 and allocated initally to Longsight (9A), the engine spent lengthy spells at Preston (24K) and Upperby (12B), moving finally to Nuneaton (2B-5E) during December 1960. Withdrawal from service took place on 8th June 1962. *Ray Farrell*

73

(Above) Leaving Euxton Junction behind, Stanier Princess Royal Class '8P' 4-6-2 No **46210** *Lady Patricia* heads south with a lengthy Glasgow – Birmingham train on 11th April 1959. Above the engine's tender can be noted the roof of the old station house at Euxton whilst to the extreme left of the picture is the parapet to Euxton Lane bridge (No 91), again a structure resulting from the quadrupling. The engine was a Polmadie (66A) locomotive at this time, having originally been allocated briefly to Crewe North (5A) when new, before moving to Camden (1B) for a seven and a half year stay. The locomotive moved from Polmadie to Kingmoor (12A) in March 1961 and was withdrawn from there on 6th October 1961.

(Centre) LMS built Class '4F' 0-6-0 No **44265** of Sheffield Grimesthorpe (41B), heads a southbound empty stock working - more than likely from Blackpool - on the Up Fast line between Euxton Junction and Balshaw Lane & Euxton station on 25th July 1959. During the summer timetable it was not unknown for these workhorses to bring seasonal trains across the Pennines and then be utilised for duties such as this. There is a distinct possibility that the train, made up of compartment stock, was bound for Springs Branch for servicing before retracing its steps for the return trip. The '4F' had returned to 41B on 3rd January 1955, a depot where it had previously been based for nearly six years before moving to Burton (17B-16F) during week ending 26th July 1941. The locomotive also had spells at Gloucester (85B) and Kettering (15B), before moving to Barrow Hill (41E) from where it was withdrawn on 15th December 1963. It stayed at Grimesthorpe until September 1961. The signals to the left of the rear of the train are banner repeating signals for Euxton Junction.

(Right) Royal Scot Class '7P' 4-6-0 No **46143** *The South Staffordshire Regiment*, heads a northbound express on the Down Fast line between Balshaw Lane and Euxton Junction on 25th July 1959. With twelve or so carriages behind on the descent from the summit at Coppull Hall Sidings, there will be more than enough momentum to remind those on the footplate to keep an eye on the speed. On this occasion, the 'Scot' was operating out of Longsight but within a few months would be transferred to Bushbury (3B). Another move some twelve months later to Trafford Park was followed by a spell based at Annesley (16D) to work the GC main line. Withdrawal from service took effect during week ending 21st December 1963. All (3); *Ray Farrell*

Stanier Jubilee Class 4-6-0 No **45563** *Australia*, heads south of Euxton Junction with the 6.38am Workington Main (via Barrow) to Euston express on 25th July 1959. The Jubilee, built in August 1934 and allocated new to Preston (24K), was at this time a Patricroft (26F-9H) based locomotive and was withdrawn from Warrington (Dallam) (8B) during week ending 27th November 1965. *Ray Farrell*

CHAPTER FIVE

EUXTON JUNCTION

1 mile 570 yards north of Balshaw Lane & Euxton Station, the signal box bearing the Junction name stood alongside the Down Slow line directly overlooking the connection of the former Bolton & Preston Railway which had opened on 22nd June 1843 with the North Union line.

The box which housed an 84-lever L&NWR frame was operational until 5th November 1972. Ostensibly, a simple joining of two railways giving Bolton & Preston trains access to Preston, the move provoked fierce resistance from the ever protective North Union and a dispute between them, involving fares, running rights, station access at Preston and the levying of swingeing tolls

by the N.U. was only resolved when they took over their rival from 1st January 1844. Quadrupling of the line between Standish and Euxton in 1895 enabled L&NWR trains unfettered access into Preston.

Continuing towards Leyland, Euxton Coal Sidings signal box - 898 yards north of the junction - was situated on the easterly side of the running lines, alongside the Up Fast line and in the shadow of the then newly constructed single span Bridge No.95 which would carry the then Preston By-pass which was later to be incorporated into the M6 motorway. This box, housing a 20-lever frame, was an early casualty, being closed on 14th November 1965.

Euxton Junction, 25th July 1959. Stanier Princess Coronation Class No **46229** *Duchess of Hamilton*, heads the Down 'Royal Scot' through Euxton Junction on 25th July 1959. To the left of the engine, the line to Bolton and Manchester curves away eastwards, initially to pass the Royal Ordnance Factory at Chorley. One can well imagine the "Duchess" still moving at about 70 - 75mph across the junction to ensure the seven/eight minute timing for the 5½ mile run into Preston was adhered to. The 'Slow' lines are to the right of the picture. Built in September 1938, the locomotive, after allocation to Crewe North (5A), moved between that depot, Polmadie (66A) and Camden (1B), which was its base at this time of the photograph. The locomotive's final move was to Edge Hill (8A) during March 1961, and withdrawal from British Railways service on 10th February 1964 was ultimately followed by full restoration for main line operation.

Ray Farrell

PRESTON

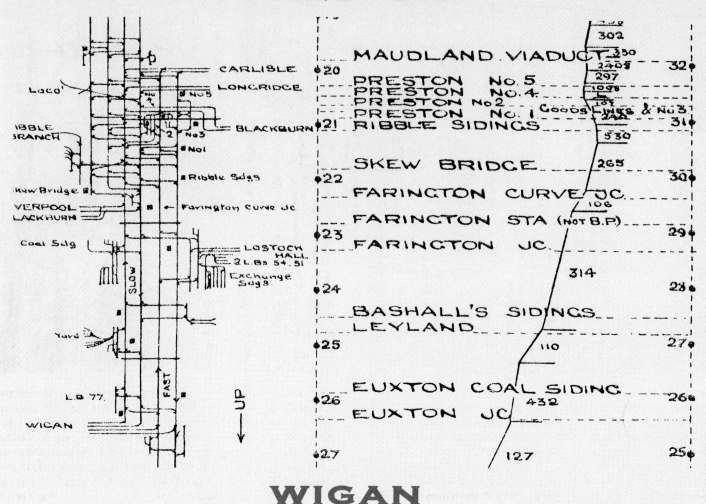

CARLISLE 20
LONGRIDGE
BLACKBURN 21

MAUDLAND VIADUCT	302 330	
	2408	32
PRESTON No.5	297	
PRESTON No.4	1098	
PRESTON No.2	102	
PRESTON No.1 Goods Lines & No3	240	31
RIBBLE SIDINGS	530	
SKEW BRIDGE	265	30
FARINGTON CURVE JC.		
FARINGTON STA (NOT B.P)	108	29
FARINGTON JC.	314	28
BASHALL'S SIDINGS		
LEYLAND	110	27
EUXTON COAL SIDING	432	26
EUXTON JC	127	25

Loco'
IBBLE BRANCH
kew Bridge
VERPOOL LACKBURN
Coal Sdg
Yard
L.B 77.
WIGAN

No5
2 No3
No1
Ribble Sdgs
Farington Curve Jc
LOSTOCK HALL 2 L.Bs 54. 51
Exchange Sdgs

SLOW
FAST
UP ↓

 20
 21
 22
 23
 24
 25
 26
 27

WIGAN

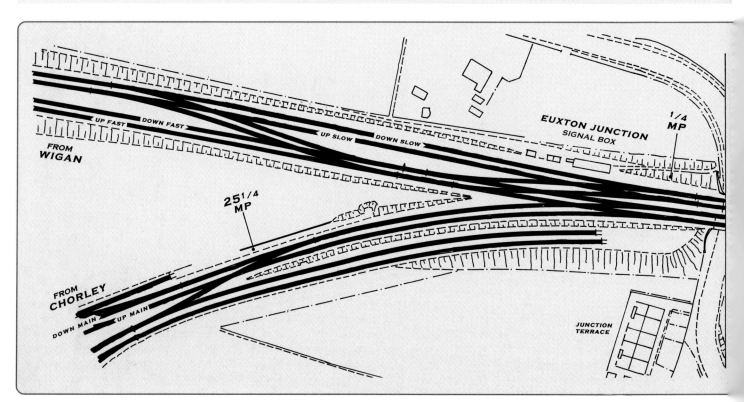

FROM WIGAN

UP FAST   DOWN FAST
UP SLOW   DOWN SLOW

EUXTON JUNCTION
SIGNAL BOX

1/4 MP

25 1/4 MP

FROM CHORLEY
DOWN MAIN   UP MAIN

JUNCTION TERRACE

Euxton Junction, 9th July 1966. Stanier Class '5' 4-6-0 No **45200** brings 1P46 the 13.00 (Saturdays Only - 18th June to 3rd September) Manchester Victoria – Blackpool North off the former Lancashire & Yorkshire route via Bolton and Chorley to join the Euston to Glasgow main line. This summer only train provided one of the quicker services on the timetable, taking 85 minutes for the 48^{1}/$_{4}$ mile journey (the 16.45 weekdays train taking 76 minutes was the fastest at the time) and included calls at Chorley, Preston, Kirkham and Poulton (for connections with the Fleetwood train, arr 14.39). However, for reasons unknown, the train has passed signals set at danger, the crew probably receiving instructions to proceed to the next signal and await instructions. 45200 was at this time allocated to Stockport Edgeley (9B), having been allocated to Crewe North (5A) when built in October 1935 and must have liked the sea air as during its 33 year life span, 10 years were spent at Southport (27C-8M),10 years at Blackpool (24E-10B) and 2^{1}/$_{2}$ years at Fleetwood (24F-10C). The locomotive was withdrawn from Carnforth (24L-10A) during week ending 20th July 1968. *Ray Farrell*

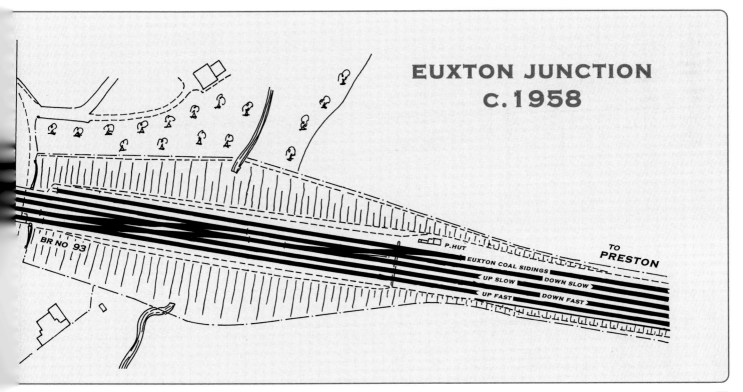

Following on from the view seen at the top of page 77, the next train to arrive on the scene was the 13.27pm ex-Manchester Victoria to Glasgow Central/Edinburgh, a summer service operating between 18th June and 3rd September. For the rest of the year (SO), the 13.27 provided something perhaps less prestigious, a non-stop service between ManchesterVictoria and Bolton! With Newton Heath's (26A-9D) Stanier Class '5' 4-6-0 No **44891** in charge the train cautiously passes Euxton Junction's Down (Bolton line) home signals, the flag carrying signalman having given the engine crew permission to proceed to the next signal. The 2-doll balanced bracket signal post to the right of the carriages carry 'boards' relating to (left) the Down Slow line and (right) the Down Fast line (to Preston). These are the Down branch 'home' signals for Euxton Junction. Beneath these signals (*See the lower picture on page 75*) were (until 14th November 1965) the corresponding 'distant' arms for Euxton Coal Sidings, next box along the line towards Preston. Following withdrawal of facilities, Euxton Coal Sidings box was closed on 14th December 1965 and the subsequent alterations involved changes to both Euxton Junction and Leyland boxes. It is likely that the 13.27 would normally take the Fast line to Preston although it is not possible on this occasion to confirm otherwise. The engine, allocated to traffic at Newton Heath on 24th August 1945 - apart from a six-week loan spell to Hellifield (24H) late in 1952 – spent its entire working life at the Manchester depot, before withdrawal during week ending 29th June 1968, just five weeks before the demise of steam on British Rail.

Ray Farrell

With Euxton Junction signal box receding into the distance, Stanier Class '8F' 2-8-0 No **48181** heads a northbound coal train along the Down Slow line towards Leyland on 5th September 1964. The signal gantry, 244 yards north of Euxton Junction box, provided support to six 'dolls', all for the control of Up trains although the gantry itself spanned four running lines as well as a Lie-bye siding on the Down side (Euxton Coal siding). The engine, built in March 1942, was initially allocated to Coalville (15D), followed by 11 years at Wellingborough (August 1944 until July 1955). At the time of the photograph, the locomotive worked out of Patricroft (26F-9H), from where it was withdrawn during week ending 19th February 1966.

Ray Farrell

(Left) Princess Royal Class 4-6-2 No **46201** *Princess Elizabeth*, passes through Euxton Junction on 25th July 1959 at the head of W67, the 11.10am (SO) Birmingham New Street to Glasgow Central (with Through carriages for Edinburgh). At the time, 46201 was a Polmadie (66A) engine, having been allocated there some twelve months earlier. It was withdrawn from service by British Railways in October 1962 whilst based at Carlisle Kingmoor (12A) and subsequently acquired by the Princess Elizabeth Locomotive Society Ltd. Initially kept at Bulmers Railway Centre, Hereford, 46201 can now be seen happily steaming around Britains railways. Euxton Junction box, to the right of the picture, contained an 84 lever LNWR tumbler frame and was situated alongside the Down Slow line, 898 yards south of Euxton Coal Siding box.

Ray Farrell

Approaching Euxton Junction on the Up Fast, Hughes/Fowler Class '6P5F' 2-6-0 No **42845**, a class first introduced in 1926 and described as *"Hughes design built under Fowler's direction"*, heads a Manchester bound passenger working on 25th July 1959. The train, Reporting No C353 was the 10.55am ex-Fleetwood to Manchester train which commenced on 27th June, connecting with the 6.30am sailing from Douglas (Isle of Man) on certain Saturdays. The gantry, supporting six 'dolls' with 'home' signals worked from Euxton Junction box, spanned the four main running lines in addition to the Down Goods Loop to the left of the picture. The extreme right hand signal is 'off' for the Bolton line where a 30mph restriction was in place for rounding the junction. The three signals to the right controlled onward movement from the Up Fast line *(from right to left)*, to Chorley and Bolton, Up Fast to Standish, Up Slow to Standish. The three signals in the 'centre' of the gantry controlled onward movement from the Up Slow line *(from right to left)*, to Chorley and Bolton, Up Slow to Up Fast (to Standish), Up Slow to Standish. The '60' sign between the Up Slow and Down Fast lines referred to the speed restriction (mph) placed on the Slow lines through the junction. The 'Crab' was based at Aintree (27B) at this time and survived until late August 1964 when withdrawn from Gorton (9G). Euxton Coal Siding is to the extreme left alongside the Down Slow line.

Ray Farrell

ISLE OF MAN
BOAT TRAINS (2)

(Left) A York (50A) Thompson Class 'B1' 4-6-0 No **61288** heads south on the Up Fast line between Leyland and Euxton Junction, with C429, the 1.15 pm Fleetwood to Manchester (Victoria) on 25th July 1959. Due to depart Preston at 1.59am, travellers on the train had already been subjected to a three hour sea crossing from Douglas (depart 9am) before disembarking into a crowded Fleetwood station. There is no doubt that arrival (Scheduled for 2.59pm) in Manchester would not come soon enough. The B1, introduced to traffic at Darlington on 16th February 1948, moved to York (50A) on 26th September the same year and spent the remainder of its working life there, before being withdrawn on 6th January 1964.

(Centre) C259, the 1.00pm Fleetwood to Manchester Victoria train, headed by 'Crab' 2-6-0 No **42707** of Newton Heath depot (26A-9D) approaches Euxton Junction on the Up Fast line on 25th July 1959, the crew preparing to negotiate the 30mph restriction imposed on trains taking the Bolton line. Another Isle of Man 'boat train', the working was not advertised in the public timetable, possibly running as a relief if required. The 2-6-0 had been at the Manchester depot since April 1947 and moved on in January 1960 to Fleetwood (24F-10C), then via Saltley (21A) to Birkenhead (6C-8H) from where it was withdrawn during week ending 19th September 1964.

(Left-lower) Midland Fowler Class '4F' 0-6-0 No **43893** heads an empty stock working southwards, taking the Up Slow line approaching Euxton Junction on 25th July 1959 probably on its way to Springs Branch. The leading pair of coaches are LMS (D2018) articulated Brake Third/Corridor Third vehicles and built originally for the 1939/40 'Coronation Scot' service. However, WW2 intervened and by the time they entered service were considered unsuitable for 'normal' use. As a result they stayed primarily in the north-west, initially being put to use on the 9am Blackpool to Liverpool service. The coaches in this scene carry British Railways post - 1956 maroon livery. 43893 moved from Hellifield (24H) to neighbour Skipton (24G) at the end of 1937 and was to remain there until withdrawn during week ending 22nd May 1965.　　All: *Ray Farrell*

All three views on this page looking in a northerly direction towards Preston show typically the overbridges built by the L&NWR over quadrupled formations. The bridge appearing over the rear of each train (No 95) was replaced by a concrete and steel structure that ultimately carried the M6 Motorway . The original bridge carried the name Rose Whittle Bridge and was just a few yards south of Euxton Coal siding signal box

On 5th July 1959, British Railways 'Clan' Class '6P5F' 4-6-2 No **72009** *Clan Stewart* heads C400, the 2.00pm Manchester Victoria to Glasgow Central away from Euxton Junction on the Down Fast line towards Leyland and Preston. The train is about to pass beneath Rose Whittle Bridge (No 95), just a short distance from Euxton Coal Sidings signal box. The train, due to pass Euxton Junction at 2.46pm, called at Bolton en-route to Preston on the initial stage of the journey. Arrival in Glasgow seemed to vary over the years but a few minutes before eight 'o' clock seems to have been pretty much the norm. A fairly sedentary scheduling took in Lancaster, Penrith, Carlisle, Beattock, Carstairs and Motherwell. The slightly rusted over rails to the right form what was Euxton Coal Sidings, effectively a Lie-Bye on the Down side. The 'Clan' was built in March 1952 and allocated to Carlisle Kingmoor (12A), where apart from a brief loan period to Stratford (Eastern Region - 30A) during September/October 1958, it was to be based until withdrawal during week ending 28th August 1965. *Ray Farrell*

(Below) Stanier Class '6P5F' 2-6-0 No **42970** of Newton Heath (26A-9D), having cleared the 1 in 110 climb away from Leyland station, passes the Euxton Coal Sidings 'home' signal (and Euxton Junction distant signals), the gradient having eased to a more moderate 1 in 432 which will see it to Euxton Junction. The train, Reporting Number W66, was the 2.00pm Morecambe Euston Road – Stockport Edgeley on 25th July 1959 and was one of the seasonal workings which were operated in conjunction with the annual 'Wakes week' holidays taken by many of the towns in north-west England. The 'Mogul' was to remain at the Manchester base only until September when it moved to Birkenhead (6C-8H) and was withdrawn whilst at Nuneaton (2B-5E) during week ending 24th October 1964. Bridge No 96 crosses the formation in the distance. *Ray Farrell*

(Right) BR Class '9F' 2-10-0 No **92233** of Carlisle Kingmoor (12A) approaches Euxton Junction on the Up Fast line with a train of hopper wagons for the ICI complex at Widnes on 9th July 1966. Running as a Class 8 freight or mineral train, some of the wagons are sheeted, indicating a load is being carried. The headcode would indicate that the train was a 'train of empties carrying a through load to a destination', some vehicles being unfitted. Euxton Coal Sidings signal box appears to the rear of the train but by this time had been closed for some months. Built in August 1958, the '9F' spent much of its early –and all too brief–working life in Wales, spending time at Pontypool Road (86G), Severn Tunnel Junction (86E), Cardiff Canton (86C-86A) and Newport Ebbw Junction (86A-86B). 92233 then followed the familiar route north to Kingmoor (12A) via Newton Heath (26A-9D) before arrival at Speke Junction (8C) on New Years Eve 1967, followed by withdrawal during week ending 3rd February 1968.

(Centre) A Newton Heath (26A-9D) based BR Class '9F' 2-10-0 No **92016** heads south with a express freight along the Up Fast line towards Euxton Junction on 5th September 1965. The bridge in the background carries the then recently constructed M6 Motorway and was designated bridge 95. The '9F' survived until October 1967, being withdrawn from Carnforth (24L-10A), just 13 years after being allocated new to Wellingborough (15A-15B) on 7th October 1954.

(Below) BR Standard Class '4' 4-6-0 No **75046** heads the 4.22pm Preston to Wigan (North Western), calling at Leyland, Balshaw Lane & Euxton and Coppull, along the Up Slow line, whilst passing under the M6 Motorway bridge on 5th June 1965. The line in the foreground is Euxton Coal Siding. Allocated new to Accrington (24A-10E) in October 1953, 75046 spent most of its relatively short working life at Bank Hall (27A-8K between Nov. 1955 and April 1966) and was withdrawn from Stoke (5D) on 6th August 1967.   All; *Ray Farrell*

(Right) Hughes/Fowler 'Crab' 2-6-0 No **42925** of Edge Hill depot (8A) heads an Up (Class 3) freight towards Euxton Junction on 5th september 1964. The signals on the left are for Down Slow line trains, the upper arm being the home 'board' for Euxton Coal Sidings, the lower being an outer distant for Leyland. The situation is repeated to the right where the signals for Down Fast trains are positioned to aid driver sighting. In this instance both Down Slow and Fast lines are cleared but the lower arms indicate caution until the next signal. The 'Coal Siding' to which the signal box gets its name is to the far left. The engine was withdrawn from Edge Hill, to where it had moved, on 8th December 1962, just two years later during week ending 28th November 1964.

(Centre) Appearing to have just enough headroom, a somewhat begrimed Stanier Jubilee Class '6P5F' 4-6-0 No **45641** *Sandwich* heads a southbound Class 4 train, possibly comprising both empty carriages and non-passenger stock along the Up Fast line, passing under the M6 Motorway bridge on 5th September 1964. To the north of the bridge abutment, Euxton Coal Sidings signal box 'peeps' out, standing adjacent to the Up Fast line. The Jubilee was allocated new to Edge Hill (8A) on New Years Eve 1934, but here at Euxton it had only two weeks of its near thirty year life to go, being withdrawn from its Burton (17B-16F) depot during week ending 19th September 1964.

(Right - lower) A case of ancient and modern amidst Lancashire surroundings on 7th June 1965 as Brush Type '4' Co-Co diesel electric No **D1813,** barely five months old, heads past Euxton Coal Sidings signal box (built 1882) with a Class 3 Empty Coaching Stock train along the Down Slow line beneath the relatively new M6 Motorway bridge south of Leyland. The 'replacement' numbering of the identification code on the loco suggests a temporary arrangement. The letter 'T' however that the working was local to Districts within the LMR. Signal box bell codes would be 2-2-1. D1813 was renumbered 47 132 under the TOPS system and in 1972 was allocated to the Birmingham Division which then included Tyseley, Saltley and Bescot. Euxton Coal Sidings box was situated 898 yards north of Euxton Junction box and contained a 20-lever frame. It was closed on 14th November 1965. All; *Ray Farrell*

EUXTON COAL SIDINGS

(Above) BR Britannia Class '7P6F' 4-6-2 No **70025** *Western Star* heads a Carlisle bound empty stock working on the Down Fast line, passing under the M6 Motorway bridge by Euxton Coal Sidings signal box on 5th June 1965. Compare the signal positions with those at the bottom of page 85. The replacements, probably LMS, have been upgraded, steel posted bracket on the left for Up Fast trains, tall latticed posted repeaters for Up Slow line trains to the right. *Western Star* was allocated new to the Rugby test plant on 13th September 1952 where it remained for 8 months before transfer to Cardiff Canton (86C-86A) on 12th May 1953. In common with many BR built locomotives, the Brittania's last move was to Carlisle Kingmoor (12A). *Ray Farrell*

(Right) A somewhat distressed looking Crewe North (5A) based Britannia Class 4-6-2 No **70052** *Firth of Tay* heads a Warwickshire Railway Society tour on the Down Fast line towards Preston on 28th November 1964. The tour, starting at Birmingham New Street, then travelled to Carlisle via Crewe, Wigan and Shap and advertised a diversity of motive power which ultimately saw 70052 on the first leg. The engine failed at Carnforth and was substituted by Class '5' No 45018 and was reported to have done well with the ten coach train. The return journey via Ais Gill from Carlisle was worked by 'Scot' No 46160 as far as Leeds. The penultimate leg from Leeds to Crewe via Standedge and Stockport was put in the hands of 'Jubilee' No 45647 *Sturdee*. *Ray Farrell*

(Right) Eastern Region Class A2, Peppercorn designed '8P7F', 4-6-2 No **60528** *Tudor Minstrel* heads 1X50, a 'circular' Manchester Exchange – Edinburgh - Manchester railtour on the Down Fast line past a now closed Euxton Coal Sidings signal box near the M6 motorway bridge south of Leyland on 23rd April 1966. The Altrinchamian Society's 'Waverley' special made the outward journey via Shap and Carlisle, returning via Newcastle, York, Leeds and Huddersfield to Manchester. Advertised motive power was A2, A4,V2 and a Jubilee. Having been introduced to traffic at Gateshead (52A) on 20th February 1948, the A2 spent the remainder of its BR working life in Scotland, moving to Dundee Tay Bridge (62B), Perth (63A), and Aberdeen (61B) from where it was withdrawn on 2nd June 1966. *Ray Farrell*

(Centre) Stanier Jubilee Class '6P5F' 4-6-0 No **45672** *Anson* heads a Manchester to Blackpool train on the Down Fast line south of Leyland on 29th August 1964. Stretching across the background is the then newly built M6 motorway, with Euxton Coal Sidings signal box visible against the bridge structure at the rear of the train. The Jubilee, built in December 1935, began its working life at Crewe North (5A) and after returning there during August 1964 completed its life cycle at the Crewe depot, being withdrawn during week ending 7th November 1964. *Ray Farrell*

(Below) Euxton Coal Sidings in LNWR days as Claughton 4-6-0 No **1319** *Sir Frederick Harrison* (LMS 5907) heads a northbound express along the Down Fast line, having just passed beneath Rose Whittle Bridge. Signal locations did not vary over the years although replacements were marginally lower. Note the ringed arms to the right, the bottom three being Euxton Juncton Up distant signals indicating the three lines available to trains from the Up Slow, i.e., *l to r,* Bolton L&Y, NU Up Fast, NU Up Slow, the higher being the Euxton Coal Sidings 'home'. They were positioned at a high level to give drivers better sighting in the case where over-bridges may have been in conflict.

H Gordon Tidey

NORTH OF EUXTON JUNCTION

(Right) Blackpool (24E-10B) Stanier Class '5' 4-6-0 No **45436** accelerates a Blackpool (North) – London (Euston) train along the Up Slow line between Leyland and Euxton Junction on 29th August 1964. The bridge (No 96) a decidedly heavier structure than the normal deep wrought iron girder type (generally Occupation bridges) commonly seen over quadrupled lines, carried road B5248 Church Road/Heald House Road from Leyland to Wigan Road and was one of the main routes to and from Leyland to the R.O.F at Chorley. The 'Black Five' was introduced to traffic at Stockport Edgeley (9B) on 16th November 1937. It's last move was to Lostock Hall (24C-10D) on 13th August 1967, withdrawal from the Lancashire shed coming during week ending 13th April 1968.

Ray Farrell

The residents of Crawford Avenue enjoyed an almost birds eye view of the railway in the shallow cutting that commenced just south of leyland as Wigan Springs Branch (8F) Stanier Class '4' 2-6-4T No **42647** heads the 12.20pm Preston to Wigan (North Western) local on the Up Slow line towards Euxton Junction on 29th August 1964. The headlamp indicating that this is an ordinary passenger train is now affixed to a lower position on the smokebox door in consequence of overhead electrification. The Stanier tank, built in December 1938 and allocated briefly to Accrington (24A-10E), spent its entire working life in the north-west, enjoying spells at Lostock Hall (24C-10D), Newton Heath (26A-9D) and Agecroft (26B-9J), before moving from Springs Branch to Birkenhead (6C-8H) during July 1966, followed by withdrawal from the Merseyside depot during week ending 13th May 1967. *Ray Farrell*

(Right) BR Standard Class '7P6F' 4-6-2 No **70030** *William Wordsworth* of Crewe North (5A), heads a southbound express freight on the Up Fast line south of Leyland on 29th August 1964. Having seen better days in its short life, the Britannia, like other latter day classes, is witnessing a quick demise in it's fortunes. Built in November 1952 and allocated new to Holyhead (6J), the 'Britannia' had a working life of less than 14 years, being withdrawn from Carlisle Upperby (12B) during week ending 25th June 1966.

(Centre) BR 'Clan' Class '6P5F' 4-6-2 No **72006** *Clan Mackenzie* heads a southbound Class 4 express freight, albeit with different headcode than that seen above (which is Class 5 coding), on the Up Fast line between Leyland and Euxton Junction on 5th September 1964. The 'Clan', having become one of the unkempt many, was built in February 1952 and initially allocated to Carlisle Kingmoor (12A). It was withdrawn from the Carlisle depot during week ending 21st May 1966 having spent all of its working life there except for a six month loan period to Edinburgh Haymarket (64B) from 25th October 1957 to 17th April 1958.

(Below) Apparently, giving its all, Crewe North (5A) based 'Britannia" Class 4-6-2 No **70029** *Shooting Star* passes the same spot, this time on the Up Slow line with its southbound parcels working on 24th April 1965, evidence of another example of the decline in overall maintenance

All; *Ray Farrell*

(Right) A Birkenhead (6C-8H) Class '8F' 2-8-0 No **48323,** operating as a Class 5 express freight heads it's train of 'Shell-BP' vacuum braked tank wagons along the Up Fast line between Leyland and Euxton Junction on 24th April 1965. Note the 'barrier' between engine and train in the form of a Brake van. Built in April 1944, the '8F' was allocated new to Polmadie (66A) before moving on to Perth (63A) and then Rose Grove (24B-10F) in July 1946. It was to the Lancashire depot that 48323 returned in May 1965, remaining there until the end of June 1968 – just five weeks before the closure of the depot – following the withdrawal of steam from British Railways on 4th August 1968.

(Centre) Britannia Class 4-6-2 No **70033** *Charles Dickens* of Crewe North (5A), heads south on the Up Slow line near Leyland with a Class 8 freight (a train of empties with some through load to a destination) of light-weight proportions on 28th November 1964. Built in December 1952, the Britannia was allocated new to Holyhead (6J), quickly moving on to Longsight (9A) for a seven year resi-dence. By June 1965 the locomotive had moved on to Kingmoor (12A) and was withdrawn from the Carlisle depot during week ending 15th July 1967. 70033 was cut up in June 1968 at G.H.Campbell, Airdrie.

(Above) A lengthy southbound express freight (Class 4 headlamps) headed by a remarkably clean Stanier Class '5' No **45034** strides along the Up Fast towards Euxton Junction on 5th June 1965. Introduced to traffic on 15th September 1934 at Crewe North (5A) the engine was at this time a Speke Junction (8C) locomotive and was withdrawn from there by early 1968. Bridge No 96 is once again in the background.

All; *Ray Farrell*

(Above) Passing through the southern outskirts of Leyland, Stanier Class '5's make their presence felt as to the right, on the Up Fast line, No **45019** of Wigan Springs Branch (8F) accelerates towards Euxton Junction with an express for London Euston. Sister engine No **44759** of Crewe North (5A) takes advantage of the falling gradient of the line along the Down Slow with a train for Blackpool on 5th September 1964. Although 45019 was introduced to traffic at Crewe North on 21st May 1935, it was some twelve years before 44759 made its debut at Perth (63A) in September 1947. Both locomotives were withdrawn during 1967, the former from Springs Branch, the latter from Carlisle Kingmoor (12A). *Ray Farrell*

(Below) BR Standard Class '9F' 2-10-0 No **92058** of Warrington Dallam (8B), heads a lengthy southbound Class 3 freight on the Up Fast line south of Leyland on 5th June 1965. It is most certainly a partially fitted (braked) train with a goodly proportion of the vacuum fitted vehicles next to the engine The locomotive, already devoid of its smokebox numberplate, was built in October 1955 and allocated new to Toton (18A-16A). After a brief spell at Speke (8C), 92058 moved to Carlisle Kingmoor (12A) on 7th August 1967 and was withdrawn from there during week ending 4th November 1967. Once again we see in the distance the stack of the chimney at Bashalls Mill, just north of Leyland station. Another feature which appears in other pictures taken from the Down Slow side at this location is the neat and tidy cess with newly installed drainage and ballast shoulder to be envied. *Ray Farrell*

(Above) Britannia Class 4-6-2 No **70028** *Royal Star* rekindles memories of better days with a Crewe train on the Up Fast line as it spiritedly climbs away from Leyland on 24th April 1965. In the distance, sister locomotive No 70029 *Shooting Star* appears to be making strenuous efforts to catch up as it heads a southbound parcels on the Up Slow line. Both locomotives were allocated to Cardiff Canton (86C-86A) within eight days of each other in late 1952, and were to be withdrawn from Carlisle Kingmoor (12A), 70028 during September and 70029 following in October of 1967.

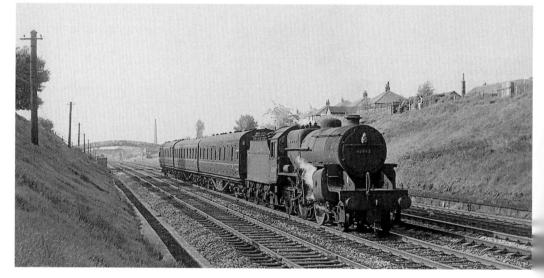

(Centre) More motive power variety on the Preston to Wigan (North Western) local passenger service, this time in the form of Hughes/Fowler 'Crab' 2-6-0 No **42942**, as it steams freely, and no doubt easily, along the Up Slow line towards Euxton Junction on 5th June 1965. More evidence of tidying up the cess and drainage with ballasting in a very orderly fashion. Allocated to Stockport Edgeley (9B) at this time, No 42942 moved to Birkenhead (6C-8H) during March 1966 and was withdrawn from the Merseyside depot during week ending 21st January 1967.

(Right) Newton Heath (26A-9D) based Class 8F 2-8-0 No **48318** with a couple of bogie bolster wagons - on which appear to be concrete beams - heading north towards Leyland (and beyond) on 22nd May 1965.

All; *Ray Farrell*

Once again, motive power well capable of the load in hand as Stanier 2-cylinder Class '4' 2-6-4T No **42631** takes a Preston to Wigan (North Western) local on the Up Slow line a few minutes after leaving Leyland on 5th September 1964. Development of Leyland south of the station had seen much new housing in the area and the curved concrete footbridge across the background provided much improved access to schools in the Turpin Green district. Whether residents of Hargreaves Avenue (on the left) and Wrights Field (on the right) appreciated the new flow in pedestrian traffic remained to be seen. However, 42631 was introduced to traffic at Southport (27C-8M) on 13th September 1938 and after spells at Bolton (26C-9K), and Newton Heath (26A-9D), moved to Wigan during April 1941. The locomotive was withdrawn from Springs Branch (8F) during week ending 12th September 1964. ***Ray Farrell***

With a maximum permissible speed on main and fast lines of 90mph, the temptation to 'open up' on the 5½ mile downward grade from Euxton Junction to Preston must have presented an exhilarating feeling for engine crews and anyone in the vicinity of Leyland station. The Fast line platforms at Leyland were the lesser used of the four and so predictably one could view the spectacle of speeding trains from relative safety. Our photographer has chosen the overbridge carrying Leyland Way, a short distance south of the station, to capture Blackpool 'Jubilee' 4-6-0 No **45571** *South Africa,* a long time resident of the depot, rapidly approaching the station on the Down Fast with an express train of considerable length, looking very impressive with a train of Crimson and Cream liveried BR Standard coaches (c.1958). Notice that the footbridge in the above picture has yet to appear in what would be followed by further encroachment by housing as the district developed. ***J Yates***

(Right) BR Standard class '9F' 2-10-0 No **92075** heads a Class 8 train comprising both tarpaulin sheeted vacuum braked hopper wagons and empty unfitted hopper wagons away from Leyland along the Up Fast on 28th May 1966, their destination possibly being Widnes. 92075 had a working life of barely 10 years 7 months, withdrawal from Carlisle Kingmoor coming during week ending 17th September 1966.

(Centre) BR Standard Class No **92009** heads north towards Leyland along the Down Slow line with a train of 'Covhops' (covered hopper wagons) on 5th June 1965. The wagons are thought to contain soda ash, part of a flow of traffic between Northwich and Corkickle (West Cumberland). The '9F' was at this time allocated to Carlisle Kingmoor (12A), having started life in March 1954 at Wellingborough (15A-15B). 92009 moved on to Carnforth (24L-10A) on New Years Eve 1967, being withdrawn from there during week ending 23rd March 1968.

(Below) The Up Slow line south of Leyland sees Britannia Class 4-6-2 No **70052** Firth of Tay heading a lengthy southbound freight on 22nd May 1965. One of the later built members of the class fitted with the high-sided tender, *Firth of Tay* appropriately spent its early days north of the border being allocated to Polmadie (66A) when built in August 1954. The locomotive was based at Crewe North (5A) at this time, moving the short distance to Crewe South (5B) the day after this working. The engine's final move was to Carlisle Kingmoor from where it was withdrawn by 1st April 1967. All: ***Ray Farrell***

(Right) Britannia Class No **70051** *Firth of Forth,* here performing the task originally intended for her, accelerates south away from Leyland, taking the Up Fast line with a Blackpool – London Euston express on 22nd May 1965. Entering into traffic 10 days before sister engine No **70052,** the Britannia followed a similar route, starting life at Polmadie (66A) before periods at Corkerhill (67A), Crewe North (5A), Crewe South (5B), Banbury (84C) and finally Carlisle Kingmoor (12A). Withdrawal from the Carlisle depot came during week ending 16th December 1967. *Ray Farrell*

CHAPTER SIX
LEYLAND STATION AND APPROACHES

With a population of about 3,500 when the North Union line through the town was opened in October 1838, compared to its northerly neighbour Preston with some 23,000 inhabitants, Leyland's status as a rail centre was relatively insignificant.

Some early records indicate that the station was initially called Goldenhill although this name lasted barely one year before becoming Leyland.

Nevertheless the station survives today, serving a town with some 25,000 residents and which over the intervening years has seen the development and in some instances the decline of a variety of industries including Commercial Vehicle Manufacture, Textiles, Rubber and Paint.

The station comprised 4 platforms with a central island and 2 outer platforms; Main line through traffic used platforms 4 (Up Fast) and 3 (Down Fast) with platforms 1 and 2 servicing the stopping trains.

Leyland station signal box was actually located some 100 yards north of the station between the Down Fast and the Up Slow lines, and housed a 30-lever LNW tumbler frame. It was closed on 5th November 1972, just ten years short of a century of service

On the westerly or Down side of the running lines directly across from the signal box was Leyland Goods Yard. In addition to the usual offices and storerooms the substantial area occupied, embraced a goods warehouse, 10-ton crane and what at one time would have been the obligatory cattle pen. The sidings closed on 19th January 1969.

562 yards north of Leyland, Bashalls Sidings signal box stood adjacent to the Down Slow line just beyond the Leyland Motor complex. It was also an early casualty closing on 4th October 1965.

A number of bridges crossed the quadruple track between Leyland and Preston, the most conspicuous being bridge No.102 carrying Centurion Way with its single span of 47'-6".

(Left) Returning with a train of empty 'Covhops', Stanier Class '5' 4-6-0 No **45128** intensifies its efforts to climb south towards Euxton Junction along the Up Slow on 22nd May 1965. This long train of 'Empties' bound for St Helens (Clock Face), had left Corkickle at 7.25am (previously 7.15) and retimed. From here, the working travelled via the Whelley line from Standish Junction and since the 1st March the train had been reclassified 4. Built in May 1935, No 45128 had a nomadic existence, having four different bases in its first 5 months – Crewe North (5A), Holyhead (6J) Llandudno Junction (6G) and Wigan Springs Branch (8F) before moving to Edge Hill (8A) in March 1936 for a seven year stay. A Crewe North locomotive again at this time, 45128 returned to Springs Branch (8F) on 18th July 1965 and was withdrawn from the Wigan depot during week ending 10th September 1966. *Ray Farrell*

In the final months of its working life, Royal Scot Class '7P' 4-6-0 No **46140** *The King's Royal Rifle Corps*, already relegated to more mundane duties than befitting its pedigree, heads south through Leyland, taking the Up Slow line with a mixed freight on 5th June 1965. Carrying the headcode for a Class 5 express freight, it is a little surprising that the lamp bracket at the top of the smokebox door has not being repositioned to a lower level in consideration of the expanding overhead electrification network. Perhaps however the loco's days on express duties resulted in the modification not being carried out. As one of the last of its class to be active in the north west, the "Scot" spent the last 12 months of its working life at Carlisle Kingmoor (12A), before withdrawal during week ending 30th October 1965. *Ray Farrell*

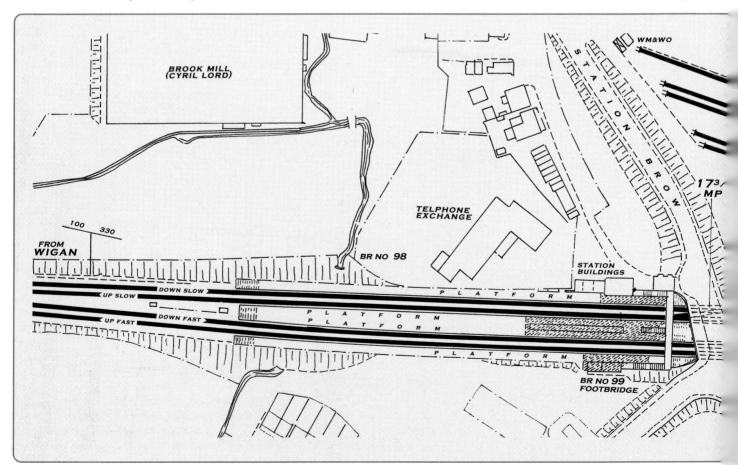

Carrying the headcode for a Class 8 freight, Stanier Class '5' 4-6-0 No **44819** clears platform 2 at Leyland heading a southbound train along the Up Slow line in readiness for the short section up a 1 in 110 gradient on 14th May 1966. The Class '5' was a Warrington Dallam (8B) resident at this time, having spent more than 14 years at Derby (17A-16C) in three spells and having moved to Wigan Springs Branch (8F) during May 1967, was withdrawn from there during week ending 2nd December 1967.

Ray Farrell

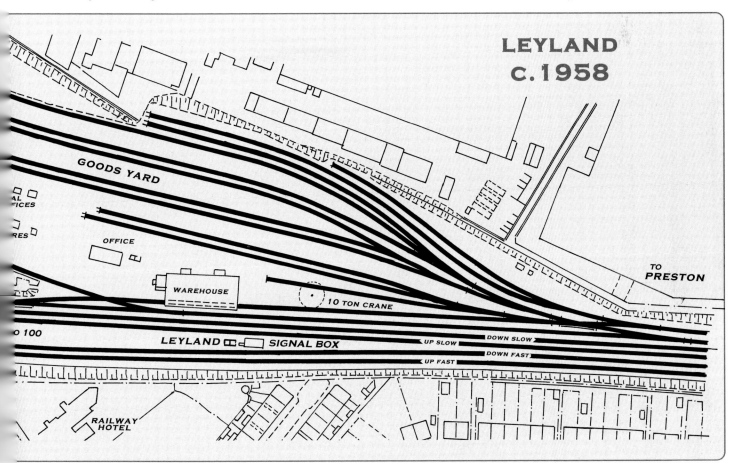

(Above) It never rains without it pouring as the continous appearance of super powered locomotives in such a short space of time make their presence felt at Leyland. This time, Stanier Princess Royal Class 4-6-2 No **46201** Princess Elizabeth (seen earlier in the book at Euxton Junction) passes alongside platform 3 on the Down Fast line with a Birmingham (New Street) to Glasgow (Central) train on Saturday 13th August 1958.

(Centre) A typical Lancashire downpour welcomes the Down 'Royal Scot' rushing though Leyland's platform 3 headed by Stanier Princess Coronation Class '8P' 4-6-2 No **46247** City of Liverpool on 13th August 1958. The Stanier Pacific spent the first 18 years of its working life at Camden (1B) having been allocated to the north London depot when new in September 1943. The locomotive was withdrawn from Carlisle Kingmoor, its only other base, on 25th May 1963.

(Right) One can guarantee that there will be young boys about to witness activity such as this provided by Camden (1B)'s Royal Scot Class '7P' 4-6-0 No **46116** *Irish Guardsman* as it bursts from beneath a smoke filled Station Brow bridge (No100) at the head of a Perth to London (Euston) express alongside Leyland's rain soaked platforms on 13th August 1958. The climb to Euxton Junction is now well and truly on for the nomadic 'Scot', originally allocated to Crewe North (5A) in October 1927. It later had spells at Camden (1B), Holyhead (6J), Llandudno Junction (6G), and Edge Hill (8A) before withdrawal from Carlisle Kingmoor on 16th August 1963.

All: *Ray Farrell*

The immense bulk of Stanier 'Duchess' 4-6-2 No **46226** *Duchess of Norfolk* heads south through Leyland taking the Up Fast line with the 9.0am Perth to London (Euston) express on 23rd May 1959. Departure from Preston was scheduled for 3.2pm with an arrival in Euston at 7.35pm after calling at Crewe and Rugby. Through carriages from Workington (Main) and Whitehaven, routed via Barrow, were attached at Preston. Despite nationalisation in 1948 and the implementation of the 1955 Modernisation Scheme, the railway outwardly had not altered much. New rolling stock and a start to electrification yes, but the infrastructure and minor items such as station furniture was still very much a collection of LNWR and LMS. Leyland was still very much an LNWR station and looked it. The LMS and possibly BR in its infancy had slightly improved matters. Electric lighting and periferals such as boundary and platform fencing would have little effect. The platform seating had its origins with a Derby foundry, probably painted in the same maroon colours that BR had sought to impose with station signing. To the right of the picture are houses built by the LNWR, standard types seen throughout the system. It would be 1972 with commissioning of the Weaver Junction to Glasgow electrification that eventually brought dividends. Reverting to motive power, one of the earlier built Stanier Coronation Pacifics, No 46226 was allocated new to Camden on 23rd May 1938. Moving to Carlisle Upperby (12B) for its fourth visit, during week ending 20th October 1956, the locomotives final move was to neighbouring Kingmoor (12A). Withdrawal came during week ending 12th September 1964, followed by scrapping at West of Scotland Shipbreaking – Troon.

Right) Normally the domain of 'Crabs' or such like but obviously an occasion when it was 'all hands to the pumps' judging by the appearance of a rather sad looking BR Standard Class '9F' 2-10-0 No **92016**, at this time a Newton Heath (26A-9D) locomotive, at the head of C801, a Central Division special to Blackpool. The special, comprising what appears mainly to be compartment stock, rolls alongside Leyland's platform 3 on 23rd May 1959, perhaps somewhat flattered by its express passenger train headcode. Built in October 1954 and allocated new to Wellingborough (15A-15B), No 92016 spent some nine of its 13 year life at Newton Heath before moving to Carnforth (24L-10A) during June 1967 and was withdrawn from here during week ending 21st October 1967 before scrapping at Motherwell Machinery & Scrap, Wishaw.

Both: *Ray Farrell*

LEYLAND

(Right) A Carlisle Upperby based Stanier Class '5' 4-6-0 No **44937** passes through Leyland station's platform 4 on the Up Fast line with a Blackpool – London Euston train on 5th June 1965. As few local trains used this platform, some rationalisation of buildings has taken place and although the main buildings are at road level and on platforms 1 to 3, they are beginning too look somewhat weatherbeaten. The building to the left has the appearance of North Union origin, not dissimilar to the Grand Junction stations some distance south, the rest of the buildings are add-ons by the LNWR. Needless to say, the station is still fully operational over four decades later. The tall co-acting signals of lattice post construction, were needed because of the numerous overbridges in the area and provided to overcome sighting difficulties experienced by drivers of approaching trains. The wooden structure at road level to the left of the semaphores still remains, housing the station entrance and booking hall. No 44937, built in November 1945 and allocated to Longsight (9A), moved briefly to Crewe South (5B) and then Walsall (3C) before returning to the south Manchester depot at the end of October 1948 where it remained for twelve years. The locomotive was finally withdrawn whilst at Carlisle Kingmoor during week ending 13th May 1967. *Ray Farrell*

(Centre) It is New Years Eve at Leyland in 1964 but the station does not appear to be very much in the festive spirit. The photograph however shows Platform 1 and the original 'main' buildings that served the station until the line was quadrupled in 1882. Until that time, a level crossing had enabled direct access to platform level. Subsequently, the new road which was built to bridge the railway resulted in a new entrance at the higher level and is seen here abutting the earlier building which contained the Station Masters House. *G Biddle*

(Right) Summer timetable working, displaying Reporting No 2P64, the 11.15am Manchester (Victoria) to Blackpool (North) and headed by Stanier Class '5' 4-6-0 No **44846,** passes through Leyland station along the Down Fast on 9th July 1966. This was a train some would describe as 'semi-fast', its first call being Bolton. Obviously intended for holidaymakers, further calls were then made at Lostock Junction, Blackrod, Adlington Chorley and Preston (omitting Leyland). Further stops were scheduled at Kirkham (for connections to Lytham and Blackpool South) and Poulton (for Fleetwood). Introduced to traffic on 11th November 1944 at Kentish Town (14B) where it remained for nearly 18 years, the locomotive when photographed here had moved north to Newton Heath in July 1965. Withdrawn whilst at the Manchester depot during week ending 13th January 1968, 44846 ended its days at Draper's (Hull), being cut up before the end of April 1968. *Ray Farrell*

The signalman at Leyland will most certainly be getting a box full of sulphurous fumes from Blackpool's (24E-10B) Stanier Class '5' 4-6-0 No **45238** if this photograph is anything to go by. The signal box door has been no doubt left open to accommodate seasonal temperatures, the 'bobbie' in the process of recording the passage of the train prior to lowering the passed signals to danger once again. The brick structure to the left of the picture is the goods yard warehouse, a sizeable building containing no less than four 30cwt cranes for internal transshipment of goods from rail to road (outside). The 'Black Five' is passing through Leyland on the Up Slow line with a southbound express from Blackpool on 29th August 1964. Built in 1936, it was initially allocated to Chester (6A) and after several spells in Yorkshire at Huddersfield (55G), Grimesthorpe (41B) and Holbeck (55A). Shortly afterwards, 45238 moved to Warrington Dallam (8B) during week ending 5th September 1964, its final home prior to withdrawal in December 1966. *Ray Farrell*

Both BR Standard Classes and the ubiquitous LMS Stanier Class '5' 4-6-0's were now well entrenched in the process of running down steam traction on British Rail, leading to a situation where all but the most recently built of motive power survived. A view typical of this period sees Class '5'No **45449** (8F-Wigan Springs Branch) heading south past Leyland station signal box along the Up Fast line with a fitted freight on 5th June 1965. The engine had been introduced to traffic at Crewe North (5A) on 14th December 1937, and after moving to Wigan Springs Branch from nearby Preston (24K) during week ending 11th April 1942, spent the next 25 years at the Wigan depot before withdrawal during week ending 2nd December 1967. What must be noted again is the neat and tidy 'ten-foot' between Up Slow (left) and Down fast (right) lines, a credit to the local Permanent way gangs. Getting nearer by each photograph is the chimney stack of Bashalls Mill, seen so many times on our approach to Leyland. To residents of Boundary Street (immediately behind the train) it would no doubt be just part of the 'scenery'. *Ray Farrell*

BR Britannia Class '7P6F' 4-6-2 No **70030** *William Wordsworth* passes through Leyland on the Up Slow line with a short southbound empty stock train comprising both non-passenger and freight vehicles on 5th June 1965. To the left in front of the warehouse is access to the small cattle dock which at one time had served Leyland's livestock requirement. The goods yard with a total of eleven sidings of miscellaneous lengths, were beyond the warehouse. Despite the fact that public facilities were not withdrawn until November 1968, the warehouse is in some disrepair, suggesting minimal use although it still retains its red and white 'Limited Clearance' plates either side of the doors. What should be noted is the 'gallows' bracket affixed, unusually, to the side of the warehouse wall and from which was suspended at one time the loading gauge. Leyland station signal box, some 100 yards north of the station, is visible above the rear of the train. The 'Britannia' started life at Holyhead (6J) on 19th November 1952. At the time of this photograph however it was allocated to Crewe South and after moving on to Upperby on 18th July 1965, was withdrawn from the Carlisle depot during week ending 25th June 1966. *Ray Farrell*

A Blackpool to Crewe train, with Class '5' 4-6-0 No **44684** in charge, proceeds along the Up Fast line past Leyland station signal box on 5th June 1965. Situated in the 'ten-foot' between the Slow (left) and Fast (right) lines, the box was located some 100 yards north of the station and dated from 188, containing a 30-lever LNWR Tumbler frame. We are now getting a clear outline of Bashalls Mill and the prominent chimney structure. The locomotive was introduced to traffic at Crewe North (5A) on 14th July 1950 and spent some 14 years there. Withdrawal came during week ending 16th September 1967 from neighbouring South shed to where it had moved during September 1964. *Ray Farrell*

Despite its external condition, Stanier Princess Coronation Class '8P' 4-6-2 No **46248** *City of Leeds* heads quite majestically an Up express on the Fast line past Leyland Station signal box on 29th August 1964. A busy Leyland goods yard with its 10 ton crane prominent, services coal wagons located on the two shorter sidings behind the warehouse. Freight operation into and from the yard came under the authority of the Preston Divisional Manager and serviced via one of the 'shunt' trips to and from Greenbank to the north of Preston. Traffic latterly had been in the hands of an afternoon trip (9T12) from Preston NU yard (dep 15.00), arrival at Leyland being scheduled for 15.15. Shunting or other yard requirements lasted until 18.06, when departure, initially for Farington Junction (18.14 - 18.30), was followed by periods at Ribble Sidings (18.42 - 19.08), Greenbank (19.27) and Oxheys (19.30). This arrangement did not include Saturdays. There was also a daily working (from Preston NU- dep18.05) to Warrington Extension Sidings, arriving at Leyland (18.17) and shunting as required before departure at 18.44. The yard was closed in November 1968 to the public but remained in use as Private Sidings. The Stanier Pacific was at this time based at Crewe North where it spent much of its working life. Within a week of this photograph, *City of Leeds* was withdrawn from traffic.

Ray Farrell

There is something different and quite special about a 'Crab' at speed. Here, sweeping along the Down Fast line just north of Leyland station shows Hughes/Fowler 6P5F No **42715** of Gorton (9G), probably not now at its best but showing a nice turn of speed with 1X13, an unidentified inter-regional special probably bound for Blackpool on 29th August 1964. The 'X', introduced in June 1961 when the four-position train identification system came into being, may well have assisted railway staff but it almost totally confused the layman or enthusiast. To the right is what appears to be a strangely quiet Leyland goods yard, in complete contrast to the view above, taken on the same day but from a different angle. The empty sidings remind us of the one time requirement of places such as Leyland.

Ray Farrell

(Right) English Electric Type '4' No **D288** heads 1A33, the 8.40am Carlisle to London (Euston) along the Up Fast line, passing Bashalls Sidings signal box on 29th August 1964. The signal box, situated adjacent to the Down Slow line 562 yards north of Leyland and 1626 yards south of Farington Junction was an early casualty, being closed on the 4th October 1965. There had been much track rationalisation in the vicinity, evidenced by the disturbed ballast and the removal of points, crossings and the line in the right foreground which had been the siding to Bashalls Mill. D288, introduced in August 1960, ultimately became 40 088 under the T.O.P.S scheme. It was withdrawn in February 1982. *Ray Farrell*

(Centre) Stanier Class '5' 4-6-0 No **45248** heads a northbound freight on the Down Slow line past Bashalls Sidings signal box on 24th April 1965. Bashalls box was a very short distance north of Leyland, bisected by an overbridge which connected Mill Street with Carr Lane. The rationalisation of trackwork formerly under the control of Bashalls, replaced by plain lines, can clearly be seen in this view south from another overbridge, this one carrying what is now Centurion Way. The layout of a few years previously is seen in the diagram below. Introduced to traffic on 21st September 1936 at Holyhead (6J) the Class '5' spent four years at Crewe South (5B), from September 1944 to December 1948, to where it was to return in October 1960. Eventual withdrawal came whilst at the Crewe depot by the end of February 1966. *Ray Farrell*

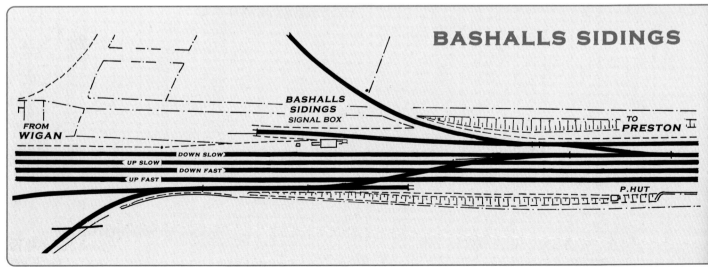

(Left) Springs Branch (8F) Stanier Class '8F 2-8-0 No 48675 heads a northbound coal train along the Down Slow line between Leyland and Farington Junction on 24th April 1965. Still on a downward grade at 1 in 314, the train has just passed beneath bridge No 102 which carries what is now Centurion Way, a point just south of the former Leyland Motors plant, the site of which fills the area to the left travelling north. The cantilevered two-doll bracket signal, probably a replacement by the LMS, became a regular feature at various locations between Wigan and Preston, the Slow line arms extended well over to make sighting straightforward. The 8F, built in March 1944, was allocated new to Nottingham (16A-16D). After a brief stay at Heaton Mersey (9F), the locomotive returned to Nottingham during August 1947 for a 17 year spell, and was withdrawn from its Wigan depot during week ending 16th September 1967. *Ray Farrell*

(Left) A Fleetwood (24F-10C) locomotive, Stanier Class '5' 4-6-0 No 44988 heads 1E53, a relief from Blackpool (North) to Barnsley (Exchange) on the Up Fast line near Leyland on 29th August 1964. In the cess lies numerous concrete fencing posts, no doubt dropped off by an engineers train for repair work to the boundary fence. Notice also the guy wires to the signal posts to give rigidity. *Ray Farrell*

(Below) With Farington Junction fast approaching, the signals give an indication of a clear road ahead for Blackpool (24E) based Stanier Class Five No 44927, steaming along the Down Fast with a semi-fast train comprising compartment stock, the likelihood being that the destination is Blackpool (c.1958). To the right is the Spurrier Works of Leyland Motors (George Spurrier was the bother of James Sumner, founder of the company which became Leyland Motors. *J Yates*

(Right) Stanier Class '5' 4-6-0 No **44982** heads 1J29, the 10.07 am. Blackpool (North)-Manchester (Victoria) on the Up Slow line near Farington Junction on 1st April 1967. The letter 'J' in the second position of the four-position train identification indicates the train is bound for a destination in the Manchester North District. Built in September 1946, 44982 was initially allocated to Leeds Holbeck (55A) and had spells at several Lancashire Depots, including Fleetwood (24F-10C) – its home at this time – before moving to Carlisle Kingmoor (12A) during week ending 18th September 1965. Withdrawal came from Kingmoor early May 1967

(Centre) Another 'Class Five', this time from Carlisle Kingmoor, sees No **45135** in full cry south of Farington Junction as it heads a southbound Class 5 express freight on the Up Fast line on 24th April 1965. Introduced to traffic on 22 May 1935 at Crewe North (5A), the Class '5' moved within a week to Patricroft (26F-9H) where it was to remain for 16 years. The locomotive moved to Carlisle Kingmoor (12A) during November 1964 and was withdrawn from there the first week in October 1967.

(Below) Stanier Class '8F' 2-8-0 No **48296** heads a train of 'Covhop' soda ash wagons on the Down Slow line near Farington Junction on 24th April 1965. There was at the time an 09.10 (7L00) Northwich to Corkickle No 1 (arr 15.59) in West Cumberland. It is perhaps worth mentioning that the last stage of the journey included rope haulage to reach the Marchon works, one of the last commercially operated inclines in the UK. The '8F' was based at Speke Junction (8C) at this time and would probably work as far as Carnforth with this train and crew. It moved briefly to Edge Hill (8A) in March 1965 but soon returned to Speke and was withdrawn during week ending 17th September 1966. All: *Ray Farrell*

(Above) To the left of the main lines at Farington Junction, the sidings had facilities for storage and marshalling, mainly of coal as we can see from the above picture, although a sizeable number of cattle wagons have somehow found there way on the scene. That was on the Down or northbound side. The exchange sidings to the right were principally for traffic to and from the former 'L&Y' lines of East Lancashire and beyond, note the rows of Brake Vans in attendance for arriving and ongoing trains that had to be re-marshalled. The elevated nature of the signal box gives an indication of the need for good sighting over a large area. Meanwhile, the main lines had to be monitored with plenty of passing trains, both freight and passenger. Here we see Class Five 4-6-0 No **44733** (10A-Wigan Springs Branch), viewed from Fowler Lane overbridge (No 103), crossing the junction on the Up Fast with a 'semi-fast' southbound passenger working on 3rd July 1965. Somewhat surprisingly, Farington Junction was an unwitting victim of its LNW/L&Y 'joint' status, details of its workings being in Working Time Tables (Freight)for the LMR (North Western Lines; Section B - Euxton Jcn and Gretna Jcn and Branches) and those for LMR (Central Lines; Section D - Clifton Junction and Blackpool and Fleetwood and Branches). Shades of the NU and ELR in the middle of the Twentieth Century. The shiny rails to the right foreground are somewhat misleading, the line was no more than a headshunt. *Ray Farrell*

Barely 1 mile north of Bashalls Sidings, Farington Junction signal box, which housed a 90-lever LNWR tappet frame dating from 1882 was situated next to the Up Fast main line.

The box controlled the main lines and adjacent westerly sidings together with the Farington Fork, which diverged north easterly immediately south of the box taking the former L&Y route towards Lostock Hall and Blackburn. The box, dating from 1882, was closed on 5th November 1972.

Although Leyland was separated from Preston by a mere 4miles and 3chains , the North Union saw fit to introduce an intermediate station at Farrington, as the original was spelt, just 1m-58ch north of Leyland.

Built to the same overall design as its neighbours, with a central island and two outside platforms, those on the west side served the slow lines, the station becoming Farington (with a single 'r') in 1857, a spelling it retained until closure, 7th March 1960.

Located less than 1/4 mile north of Farington Junction, the station was accessed at the southern end of the platforms from the Croston Road bridge, designated No 107 and comprising two spans of 25'-0".

At the northern end of the station, intersection bridges 109, with 36'-0" and 32'-4" spans, carried the former L&Y line linking Lostock Hall and Blackburn with Ormskirk, Liverpool and Preston over the main line. These intersection bridges were 'over' as far as the North Union line was concerned and 'under' in the eyes of the L&Y. On the western exit from the crossing, the route to Preston branched north to join the line from Liverpool giving access to the northbound Euston to Glasgow line (WCML) at Farington Curve.

The station was completely demolished shortly after closure, the only indication of its 122-year existence being the gap between the Down Fast and the Slow lines in which the central island platforms were located.

Approaching Farington Curve Junction, Flag Lane crossed both the North Union by bridge No.112 – a single span of 47'-5" and the former Lancashire Union line to Liverpool by bridge No. 6 – span 26'-10".

The Liverpool line, having been joined at this point by the route from Blackburn - which had crossed the main line at Farington - converged to join the main line just south of Bee Lane bridge designated No.113 and comprising three equal spans of 29'-8".

Immediately north of the bridge, Farington Curve Junction signal box, a 30-lever LNWR tumbler frame, was situated tight up against the bridge support between the Down Fast and Up Slow lines. Another structure of 1882 vintage, the box was closed on 5th November 1972.

Bridge No.114 with a single span of 49'-0" and known as 'Skew Bridge' due to the angle at which it carried the Leyland – Preston road over the main line was some 1/2 mile north of the curve junction.

Beyond that, Skew Bridge signal box, housing a 36-lever LNWR tumbler frame, was situated on the westerly side of the running tracks just 1 mile south of Preston and at the point where the through lines giving access to Ribble Sidings left the slow main lines. It was closed on 4th February 1973.

Once again, the photographer takes advantage of Fowler Lane bridge to record this southbound 'race' developing through Farington Junction. To the left, Fleetwood's (24F-10C) Stanier Class '5' 4-6-0 No **44982** bowls along the Up Slow line at the head of 1J38, the 10.35am Blackpool South-Manchester (Victoria) keeping pace with English Electric Type '4' (Class 40) 1Co-Co1 No **D339** hauling a late running 1A33, the 8.39am Carlisle-London Euston on the Up Fast through Farington Junction on 17 July 1965. The Blackpool train ran via the coast line, leaving out only Salwick on the journey to Preston. 1A33, in its 5½ hour schedule, provided an almost local service north of Crewe, including Penrith, Shap, Tebay, Oxenholme and Lancaster before reaching Preston. Wigan, Warrington, Hartford, Crewe and Stafford then preceded an unbroken spell to Bletchley prior to the Euston finale (arr. 14.00). The Class '5' was built in 1946 and allocated new to Leeds Holbeck (55A) on 17th September. After lengthy stays at Blackpool (24E-10B) and Fleetwood (24F-10C) the locomotive moved to Carlisle Kingmoor (12A) in September 1965, withdrawal coming during week ending 6th May 1967. D339, introduced to traffic in April 1961, becoming 40 339 under the T.O.P.S scheme. It was withdrawn during February 1982. *Ray Farrell*

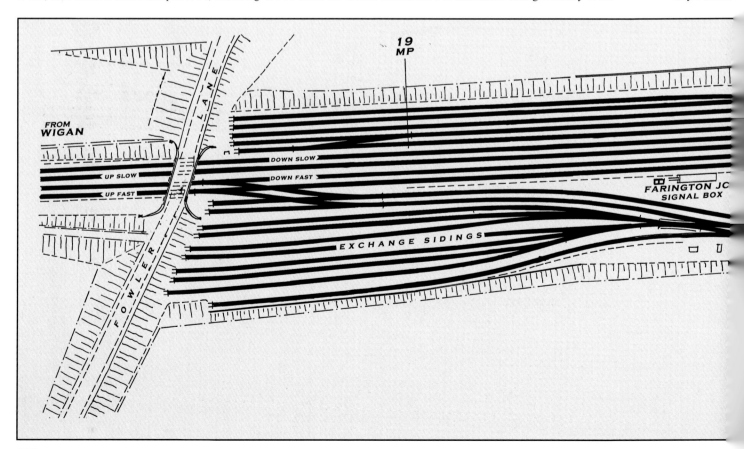

Farington Junction on 17th July 1965. A Manchester-Blackpool original Derby 'Lightweight' DMU heads north on the Down Fast whilst BR Britannia Class '7P6F' 4-6-2 No **70018** *Flying Dutchman* makes good headway on the Up Slow with 1A31, the 7.00am Workington (Main)-London Euston. The first stage of the journey from Workington was via Cockermouth and Keswick with Through Carriages to Carlisle. At this time a Crewe South (5A) locomotive, the Britannia was built in 1951 and allocated new to Old Oak Common (81A) on 25th June. Moved to Kingmoor (12A) on 11 December 1966, 70018 was withdrawn from the Carlisle Depot during week ending 24th December and was cut-up by June the following year at the Motherwell Machinery & Scrap Co.Ltd. Wishaw. Note the build up in the Down Sidings of coal empties comprising 16Ton mineral wagons. ***Ray Farrell***

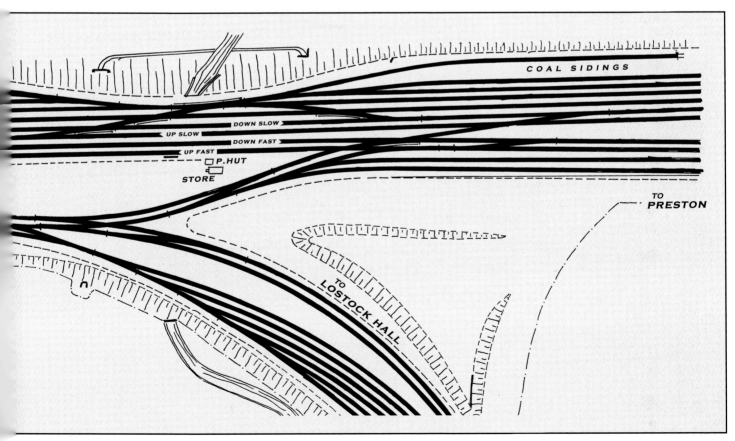

(Left) Stanier Class '5' 4-6-0 No **44863** of Edge Hill MPD (8A) heads a southbound freight on the Up Fast line past Farington Junction signal box on 28th January 1967. Built in January 1945, the Class '5' was initially allocated to Crewe North (5A) but spent most of its working life - April 1950 to January 1965 - at Rugby (2A-1F). After a brief stay at Bletchley (1E) the locomotive moved to Edge Hill on 4 July 1965, initially on loan, and was withdrawn from the Merseyside Depot on 6th May 1967, followed by cutting up at Cashmore-Great Bridge. Farington Junction Box, a 90 Lever LNW Tappet Frame was situated 1-mile 425yds north of Leyland between the Up Fast line and the Up Goods line to Lostock and Blackburn. It was closed 5th November 1972. ***Ray Farrell***

(Right) The entrance to Farington station was located off Croston Road bridge (No 107). A distinctly main line station, it never received either the service or the passengers needed to make it a going concern. Closed on 7th March 1960, it lived in the shadow of Lostock Hall station, the latter better suited to serve Preston bound passengers, the main destination for local services. Latterly it was served by five northbound (two morning, one mid-day and two evening) trains and five southbound) one in the morning and four late afternoon and evening). This view shows a returning Central Division special (c.1959) headed by Bury (26D) based Ivatt Class 2MT 2-6-0 No **46416** on the Down Slow line. The station name can just be seen above the bridge parapet over the cab of the loco. ***J Yates***

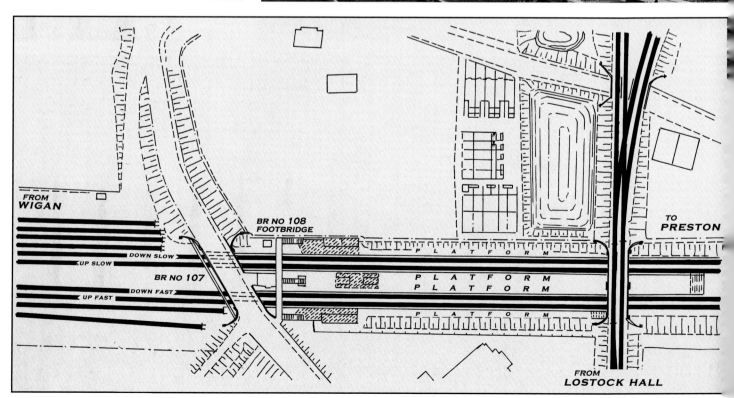

FROM WIGAN

BR NO 108 FOOTBRIDGE

TO PRESTON

DOWN SLOW

UP SLOW

BR NO 107

DOWN FAST

UP FAST

PLATFORM

PLATFORM
PLATFORM

PLATFORM

FROM LOSTOCK HALL

(Right) Hauling a train of what appear to be 'Dogfish' ballast wagons. Crewe South (5B) based Stanier 'Mogul' 2-6-0 No **42961** leaves a smoke filled bridge opening immediately to the south of Farington station. Through the bridge opening it is just possible make out the canopy over platform 2 which served the local train services between Preston and Wigan until its closure in March 1960. 49261 had been transferred from Crewe North in May 1959 and remained there for the next three years. *J Yates*

(Centre) A Carnforth (24L-10A) Stanier Class '8F' 2-8-0 No **48519** heads a southbound freight past the site of Farington Junction on 3rd July 1965. The freight is travelling on the Up Slow line and is passing under the former L&Y line from Blackburn via Lostock which connected with Liverpool to the west and also provided a northbound spur which rejoined the main line at Farington Curve Junction. As can be seen with this view and that below, Monday morning wash day was to be avoided in the gardens of Rushy Hey and Greenfield Drive. The Class '8F' which was built in 1944 and allocated new to Heaton (52B) remained in service until the end of BR steam, being withdrawn from Rose Grove (24B-10F) on 3 August 1968. *Ray Farrell*

(Below) BR Britannia Class '7P6F 4-6-2 No **70012** *John of Gaunt* accelerates the Up 'Lakes Express' past the site of the former Farington Station (Closed 7th March 1960) on 3rd July 1965, having just passed under the former L&Y line to Liverpool from Blackburn. The line also provided access to and from Preston for Lostock Hall (24C-10D), connecting with the northbound route from Liverpool at Farington Curve Junction. The Britannia spent its early years on the Eastern Division being allocated to Norwich (32A) when built in May 1951.Its final depot was Carlisle Kingmoor (12A) and withdrawal came during the last week of December 1967. *Ray Farrell*

(Right) Stanier Class '5' 4-6-0 No **45168** heads a passenger working westwards across the Euston to Glasgow (WCML) route via the former L&Y route from Blackburn to Liverpool at Farington on 3rd July 1965. The Class '5' allocated to traffic at Perth (63A) on 17th August 1935, spent its whole working life north of the border before withdrawal from St.Margarets (64A) on 26th September 1966. Its Dalry Road (64C) base at this time suggests this was a working originating in Scotland bound for Blackpool. To gain access to the coast route such workings would pass south-

bound through Preston and then travel via Whitehouse Junction, Lostock Hall and Farington Curve Junction before passing through Preston Station again – this time northbound – before taking the line to the Fylde Coast and Blackpool. The locomotive was cut up at J.McWilliam-Shettleston. *Ray Farrell*

(Centre) Stanier Class '5' 4-6-0 No **45200**, a resident at Stockport Edgeley (9B) at this time, travels light engine towards Lostock Hall (24C-10D), crossing the west coast main line at Farington on 28th January 1967. The bridge, which carried the former L&Y route from Blackburn to Liverpool over the main line and also provided access to Preston via Farington Curve Junction, comprised spans of 36'-0" and 32'-4" and was designated Bridge 109 in BR and LMS records, the number being visible on the central bridge pier. The former Farington Station (closed 7th March 1960) was located at this site, the island platform project-

ing northwards beyond the Bridge 109 pier, whilst the outside platforms terminated at the bridge. Access to the station was from Croston Road at the southern end of the platforms. No 45200 which was built in October 1935 and allocated briefly to Crewe North (5A), was withdrawn from Carnforth (24L-10A) during week ending 20 July 1968 just two weeks before the end of BR steam, and was cut up at George Cohen-Middlesborough. *Ray Farrell*

Farington. In the years just before WW1, eminent photographer H Gordon Tidey visited this location just north of Farington station, his camera focusse on L&NWR 'Claughton' Class 4-6-0 No **42** *Princess Louise* (LMS 6004) heading north with a Down London Euston to Edinburgh train. Princess Louis was rebuilt with a large boiler and was the only member of the class to survive nationalisation. It was allocated the number 46004 but never carried and was withdrawn from service in 1949. The station canopies of Farington station are to be seen in the right hand opening of the bridges although course there were platforms, four in total, on both Fast and Slow lines. *H Gordon Tide*

By 17th July 1965, the Royal Scot Class '7P' 4-6-0's were almost extinct. Here, No **46140** *The Kings Royal Rifle Corps* heads a southbound empty coaching stock train away from Flag Lane Bridge on the Up Slow line towards Farington Junction and Leyland on that date. The Liverpool branch, which forks west between the distant bridges at Farington Curve Junction is situated behind the embankment beyond the locomotive, as evidenced by the semaphores visible in front of the train. 46140 was withdrawn from Carlisle Kingmoor (12A) during week ending 30th October 1965.   *Ray Farrell*

Looking south from Bee Lane Bridge, the elevated view gives a good view of the lines from both Lostock Junction and Ormskirk (& Liverpool) as they approach Farington Curve Junction on 25th June 1966, with a Stockport (Edgeley - 9B) Stanier Class '8F' 2-8-0 No **48392** bringing a northbound Class freight across the junction on the Down Slow (NU) line from the Leyland direction. Curving away to the right under Flag Lane Bridge, the Liverpool line continues westwards to the right whilst the two lines branching left before the bridge continue in a southerly direction parallel with the Liverpool (Walton Junction) line before turning eastwards and crossing over the main (NU) line en route to Lostock Hall and Blackburn. Built in 1945, the '8F' was allocated to Kirkby (16B-16E) in April and remained there for nearly eighteen years. Withdrawn during June 1968, the locomotive had spent the last three months at Bolton (26C-9K).

Ray Farrell

With the main lines clear to the south, Brush Type '2' (Class 31/2) A1A-A1A No **D5810** brings 1M98 the 7.40am Lincoln-Blackpool (North) to join the Down Slow (NU) line at Farington Curve Junction on 25th June 1966.The train is coming off the Blackburn route having travelled via Lostock Hall and has crossed the main line some half a mile south of the junction. The Class 31 as it was to become, received the number 31 280 as part of the T.O.P.S scheme, having been introduced in August 1961. It was one of a number of the class stored in May 1981 but reinstated in January 1982.   *Ray Farrell*

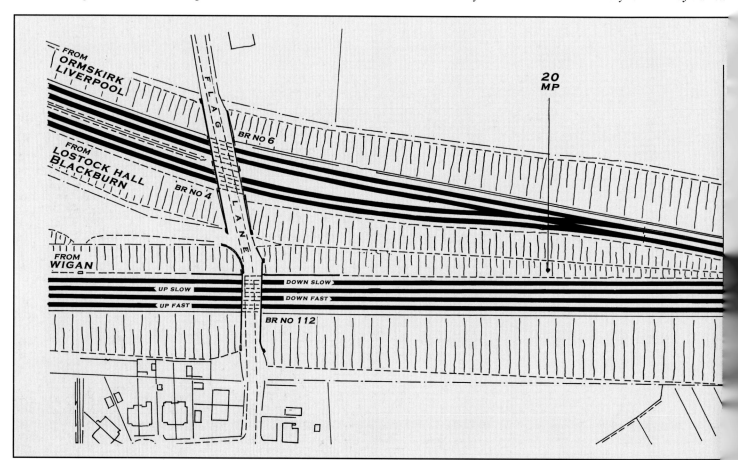

Stanier Class '5' 4-6-0 No **44915** of Lostock Hall (24C-10D) brings an unidentified passenger working through Farington Curve Junction to join the Down Slow (NU) line on 30 July 1966. The train has travelled via the Blackburn route and, photographed at 11.40am, is possibly the 7.40am Lincoln (Central) - Blackpool (North) due to pass Farington Curve at 11.24am. When built in December 1945 the Class '5' was allocated to Northampton (2E-1H) before moving to Rugby (2A-1F) during week ending 27th August 1949 where it was to spend over 15 years. Withdrawal from Lostock Hall came during week ending 9th December 1967 and the locomotive was cut-up at T.W.Ward, Beighton.   *Ray Farrell*

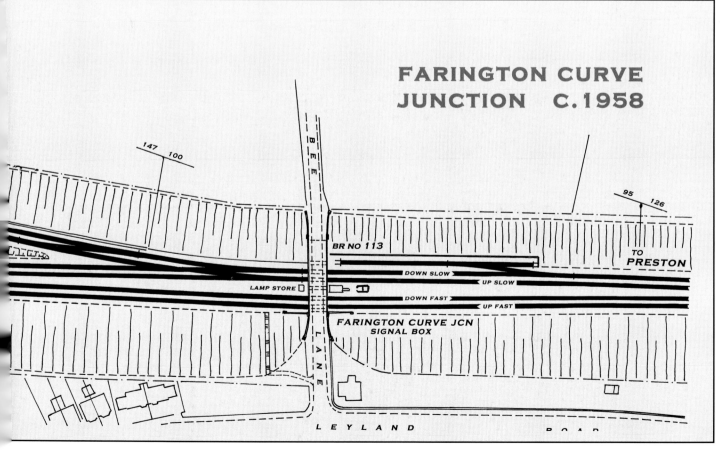

FARINGTON CURVE JUNCTION C.1958

FARINGTON CURVE JUNCTION

(Right) Stanier Class '5' 4-6-0 No **45226** heads a southbound passenger working under Bee Lane Bridge on 25th June 1966. Farington Curve Junction signal box, which remained operative until early 1973, is situated on the other (north) side of the bridge virtually up against the bridge structure between the Fast and Slow lines. The Class '5' was Lancashire based throughout its entire working life, numbering eight depots in all, starting at Southport (27C-8M) in July 1936 and terminating at Lostock Hall (24C-10D) from where it was withdrawn during week ending 16th September 1967.

(Below) BR Britannia Class '7P6F' 4-6-2 No **70031** *Byrom* gets the thumbs up from a young spotter as it accelerates under Bee Lane Bridge at Farington Curve Junction with 1Z35, a return Keswick to London (Euston) parcels special on 17th July 1965. Allocated to Holyhead (6J) when built in November 1952, 70031 then spent seven years at Longsight (9A) and eventually moved north to Carlisle, firstly to Upperby (12B) the day after this working, and then Kingmoor (12A) on 11th December 1966. Withdrawn from Kingmoor during week ending 11th November 1967, the Britannia was cut-up at J.McWilliam. Shettleston, in March 1968. Both: *Ray Farrell*

(Above) A southbound empty stock working headed by Stanier Jubilee Class '6P5F' 4-6-0 No **45604** *Ceylon*, takes the line for Moss Lane Junction and Liverpool at Farington Curve Junction on 17th July 1965. Bee Lane Bridge, comprising three equal spans of 29'-8" and designated Bridge No 113 crosses both Up and Down (NU) lines with the Junction Signal Box situated between the Down Fast and Up Slow lines. Built in 1935 and allocated briefly to Crewe North (5A) on loan, the Jubilee was on borrowed time as official records show it as withdrawn from Newton Heath (26A-9D) during week ending 17th July 1965, making this *Ceylon's* last journey. **(Below)** For such a moderate curve to and from the 'Central Lines' - as the Western Lines Sectional Appendix described the routes to Lostock Hall and Liverpool respectively - the speed restrictions of 25mph in the Down direction and 30mph in the Up (to Lostock) direction for crossing the junction seem 'cautious' to say the least. Two junctions in a short distance coupled with an ascending gradient of 1 in 100 changing to 1 in 147 required concentration, particularly with trains occasionally consisting of eight carriages and upwards. Here we see one member of the engine crew is not giving anything to chance. Both: ***Ray Farrell***

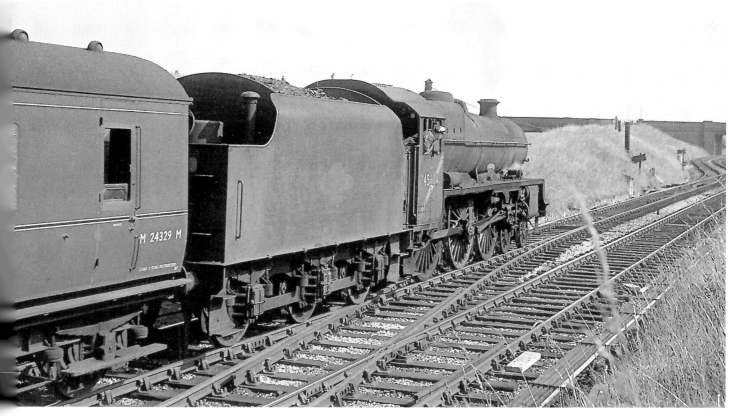

(Above) Jubilee Class '6P5F' 4-6-0 No **45721** *Impregnable* of Bank Hall (27A-8K) brings a northbound passenger working off the Liverpool line from the Moss Lane Junction direction to join the Down Slow (NU) line at Farington Curve Junction on 17th July 1965. Visible above the locomotive's tender is the Farington Curve Signal Box which housed a 30 Lever LNW Tumbler Frame and was situated between the Down Fast line and Up Slow 763 yards south of Skew Bridge Signal Box. Generally, trains from Liverpool Exchange entered Preston on the 'East Lancs' side and included Lostock Hall and Todd Lane Junction in the schedule. On Summer Saturdays however, this train was one of four that were extended to Blackpool North for the first time since the closure of Blackpool's Central Station the previous November. Running express to Aintree Sefton Arms (9 minutes), calls at Ormskirk and Burscough Junction followed before the train took the route via Farington Curve Junction to Preston. Afternoon trains would include Rufford and Croston. The Jubilee was built in 1936 and allocated to Blackpool (24E-10B) on 26th August. Moved to Bank Hall during October 1964, the locomotive was withdrawn within a year during week ending 9th October 1965.   *Ray Farrell*

(Right) A northbound freight, with express headcode and headed by BR Britannia Class '7P6F' 4-6-2 No **70036** *Boadicea*, now less nameplates, takes the Down Slow (NU) line through Farington Curve Junction whilst passing beneath Bee Lane Bridge on 17th July 1965. The Britannia Pacific was built in 1952 and allocated new to Stratford (30A) during December, before spells at Norwich (32A), March (31B), and Immingham (40B). Departing the Eastern Region 70036 moved to Upperby (12B) for a short stay and then on to Kingmoor (12A) during February 1964. Withdrawal came from the Carlisle Depot during week ending 15th October 1966. **Ray Farrell**

(Left) In lamentable external condition, ex WD Class '8F' 2-8-0 No **90395** heads away from Farington Curve Junction towards Skew Bridge with a short northbound coal train, probably bound for Ribble Sidings, on 25th June 1966. Let us hope the residents of Rookery Drive are used to the notorious 'clanking' that emanated from the motion of these engines. The 'WD' was based at York (50A) at this time after spells at Farnley (55C), Royston (55D), Normanton (55E) and Wakefield (56A), and moved finally to Sunderland (54A) just 5 days before withdrawal on 28 October 1966.

(Centre) On 25th June 1966, Upperby (12B) provided BR Britannia Class '7P6F' 4-6-2 No **70022** *Tornado* to work the 8.20am Carlisle to Birmingham (New Street) 1G14, seen here as it accelerates southwards from Preston on the Up Fast line near Skew Bridge. The letter 'G' in the identification code indicates the destination district, Birmingham. Built in 1951 and allocated to Plymouth (Laira) (83D-84A) on 16th August, the 'Pacific' had spells at Newton Abbot (83A) and Cardiff Canton (86C-86A) before moving northwards and was eventually withdrawn from Carlisle Kingmoor (12A) during week ending 11th December 1966. The locomotive was cut-up in April 1968 at Thomas Ward, Inverkeithing.

(Below) BR Standard Class '5' 4-6-0 No **73060** of Polmadie (66A) accelerates southwards away from Skew Bridge towards Farington Curve Junction, taking the Up Fast line with a Glasgow-Manchester (Victoria) train on 17th July 1965. Built in 1954 and initially allocated to Polmadie in August, No 73060 then moved to Motherwell (66B) on 25th October 1955 before returning to the Glasgow depot on 26 th August 1957. There, the 'Standard' was to remain until withdrawal on 1st May 1967.

All: ***Ray Farrell***

(**Right**) BR Standard Class '4' 4-6-0 No **75027** of Bank Hall (27A-8K) heads the 16.22 Preston to Wigan (North Western - arr 16.56) towards Farington Curve Junction on 17th July 1965. It is unlikely the identification code is applicable, 'P' being the destination code for Blackpool and Fylde District. The likelyhood is that the engine has worked into the district ealier in the day with no one minded enough to remove the chalk code. The lamp position and '2' on the smokebox do correctly indicate that it is an Ordinary Passenger Train. In the background is Skew Bridge (Leyland Road) with the signal box bearing that name visible in the distance. The 'Standard 4' spent much of its early life in the south west being allocated new to Plymouth Laira (83D-84A) in May 1954 and then enjoying spells at Reading (81D), Oxford (81F) Swindon (82C), Shrewsbury (84G), Templecombe (82G), Machynlleth (89C) and Croes Newydd (84J) before moving to Bank Hall (27A-8K) on 31st January 1965, and had been withdrawn from Carnforth by 1st August 1968.   *Ray Farrell*

(**Above**) Stanier Class '6P5F' 2-6-0 No **42960** heads south on the Up Fast line between Skew Bridge and Farington Curve Junction with a Blackpool-Manchester (Victoria) train on 17th July 1965. The Gable End Advertisement above the embankment encouraging motorists to "Put A Tiger In Your Tank" was much in evidence at the time the photograph was taken. The Stanier Mogul enjoyed a 32-year working life commencing at Willesden (1B) in December 1933 and ending in withdrawal from Heaton Mersey (9F), its base at this time, during week ending 15th January 1966. In between the locomotive experienced 25 Depot changes, its longest stay being a 6$\frac{1}{2}$ year spell at Longsight (9A) to where it moved during January 1951.   *Ray Farrell*

(**Right**) Stanier Class '5' 4-6-0 No **45446** of Crewe South (5B) at the head of a southbound freight, takes the Up Slow line passing under Skew Bridge, whilst sister locomotive No **44664** of Bolton (26C-9K) heads towards Preston on the Down Fast with a passenger working on 25th June 1966. Built in 1937 and allocated to Crewe North (5A) on 7th December No 45446 was withdrawn from its Crewe South base during week ending 11th February 1967. Although built nearly 12 years later, starting life at Sheffield Grimesthorpe (41B), No 44664 went to the cutters torch 15 months after its fellow Class '5', being withdrawn from Bolton during week ending 11th May 1968.   *Ray Farrell*

SKEW BRIDGE

(Right) In what could be described as a 'gangers eye-view', walking in the Up Slow 'four-foot' facing oncoming traffic, Skew Bridge signal box appears in the distance as the route ahead towards Preston opens up to six running lines. The street lighting from lamp standards we have become accustomed to in the Preston area once again proliferate along Leyland Road.
BR(LMR)

(Below) A Wakefield (56A) Class 'B1' 4-6-0 No **61123** heads 1X45 Morley to Blackpool North beneath Leyland Road (Skew Bridge) just a mile south of Preston on 5th June 1965. Several reverse curves, albeit of large radius chainage, made signal sighting on the approach to Preston somewhat difficult. Emerging from a long deepish cutting, abbreviated only by overbridges, Skew Bridge signal box gave an assurance that the long straight stretch into Preston was imminent, although pathing from the Down Fast to the Down Through to gain the Blackpool route on the other side of Preston station was still a little matter for the engine and crew to contend with. After its move to Wakefield on 5th January 1964, the 'B1' remained there for three years, spending its last four months at York (50A) from where withdrawal came on 11th May 1967. Skew Bridge, so named due to the acute angle at which it crossed the main line, comprised a single span of 49'-0" and was designated Bridge 114.
Ray Farrell

BR Britannia Class '7P6F' 4-6-2 No **70034** *Thomas Hardy* takes the Up Slow line with a train for Crewe on 17 July 1965, passing Skew Bridge Signal Box, 1-mile south of Preston. Immediately in front of the Signal Box, the formation widens to accommodate an additional two running lines, the Down and Up Through. As can be seen, these branch off the slow lines. Access to Ribble Sidings, situated on the west side of the lines, is from the 'Shunting Line' which connects also with the North Union Goods Yard as well as the Ribble Branch via Strand Road. The small cluster of concrete and cement/asbestos structures to the left of the signal box are of LMS origin, whilst British Railways have mounted one of their maroon enamel signs to the front of the box PRESTON - 1 MILE. The Pacific, built in 1952 and allocated to Longsight (9A) in December, had moved to nearby depot Newton Heath (26A-9D) by July 1965 and was eventually withdrawn from Carlisle Kingmoor (12A) during week ending 6th May 1967 for cutting up at J.McWilliam. Shettleton, in October 1967.

Ray Farrell

The 12.20pm (Saturdays Only) Preston-Wigan (North Western) approaches Skew Bridge with BR Class '2' 2-6-0 No **78040** taking the Up Slow line on 17th July 1965. The quadrupled main line is now supplemented by the Down and Up Through lines, principally for goods traffic and Blackpool bound traffic not calling at Preston. This local service had been a regular at this time for many years, providing connections with services from Blackpool Central/South and North trains, the former bound for Manchester, the latter with through carriages to Blackburn. As can be seen to the extreme right of the picture, Skew Bridge was popular with photographers and spotters alike, with southbound workings proving particularly atmospheric as engines striving hard on their way out of Preston in preparation for the climb to Euxton Junction. However, the summer of 1965 was the first after Blackpool Central had been closed and many of the services on that line cut back to South station. The Class '2' was introduced to traffic at Bank Hall (27A-8K) on 10th December 1954. After spells at Springs Branch (8F) and Aintree (27B-8L), the locomotive moved to Lostock Hall (24C-10D) in April 1964, and was withdrawn from the Lancashire depot during week ending 22nd January 1966.

Ray Farrell

A Patricroft (26F-9H) BR Standard Class '5' 4-6-0 No **73129** accelerates the 12.33 pm Preston-Manchester (Victoria) away from Preston on the Up Fast line towards Skew Bridge line on 17th July 1965. Note the location of the extended cantilevered signal towards the rear of the train which controlled movements on the Down Fast line. Also standing proud is the outline of the erstwhile Park Hotel, jointly owned by the LNWR and L&Y Railways and viewed particularly well by approaching trains from the south. Built in 1956 the BR Standard was allocated to Shrewsbury (84G) in August 1956 and moved to Patricroft during September 1958 where it remained until withdrawn during week ending 2nd December 1967.   *Ray Farrell*

On the approach to Preston from the south, Ribble Sidings signal box, housing a 50-lever frame, stood on the east of the running lines adjacent to the Up Fast and just south of Vignoles impressive viaduct spanning the River Ribble.

Some 750 yards further north, the huge Preston No.1. box with its 162-lever LNWR tumbler frame was similarly located next to the Up Fast just short of the station platforms. Both boxes closed on 4th February 1973.

Given the location of Preston at 209 miles north of Euston and almost exactly half-way between the Capital and Glasgow, it was perhaps inevitable that the town was to play a major role in the development of the west coast route and the linking of the two great cities.

Initial indications however were far from propitious as the station opened by the North Union as its northern terminus of their route from Parkside in October 1838 was subject to much friction and wide criticism from passengers, rail employees and local authorities alike.

The original station based on a double track with a 120' roof structure soon proved inadequate as traffic volumes increased rapidly and other companies began to use the facility.

A partial enlargement around 1850 eased the problems somewhat, but despite the addition of the East Lancashire Railway (Butler Street) section, it was evident that major improvements were essential.

Eventually a complete re-building programme under the auspices of the L&NWR and the L&Y, who had jointly taken control of the North Union with effect from 1846, was undertaken and a virtually new station opened in July 1880 at a reported cost of £200,000. The North Union as such, whilst remaining nominally a legal entity, was eventually dissolved with effect from 1st July 1888.

The main feature of the updated facility was the main island platform at 1,225 ft. long and 110 ft. wide – larger than its counterparts at Kings Cross, St.Pancras and Waterloo.

Housing platforms 5 and 6 and containing booking hall, waiting rooms and refreshment facilities, this was the centrepiece of a layout eventually providing 10 platforms plus 5 bays with a platform area of $4\frac{1}{2}$ acres within the overall site of nearly 7 acres.

Platforms 1 – 6 were utilized by the former North Union with the platforms on the easterly side, 7 – 10 serving the former ELR accessed from Butler Street.

These origins were still identified as late as the mid 1950's, when the B.R. Working Timetable (Section G) still referred to the station as Preston N.U.

Preston No.2. signal box was located in an elevated position within the station roof area, whilst platforms 5 and 6 boasted rather large 3-doll bracket signals, sited to protect crossovers in middle of the station on both Up and Down sides. At the northern end, Fishergate Bridge spanned the whole width of the station, at this point embracing 14 running lines.

In addition to the many passenger services using the station, the majority of which were scheduled to stop at Preston, an extensive freight business developed including a high volume of mail for which the G.P.O. had their own facility within the station.

Despite it's inauspicious start, the ultimate development of the station and the part played in providing facilities for the many routes converging there, well merited the name bestowed upon the town – now a city – "PROUD PRESTON".

(Right) Waiting to depart the south end of Preston's Platform 6 with a Perth to London Euston train is Carlisle Upperby's Stanier Princess Coronation Class '8P' 4-6-2 No **46250** *City of Lichfield* on 5th September 1963. *Ray Farrell*

PLATFORM 6

(Below) Stanier Princess Coronation Class '8P' 4-6-2 No **46250** *City of Lichfield* re-starts a Perth-London Euston train out of Preston on 5th September 1963. Partially hidden by the exhaust is the outline of the erstwhile Park Hotel, jointly owned at one time by both the L&NW and L&Y Railways. Built in May 1944 and allocated new to Crewe North (5A), the Pacific was to spend most of its time at Camden (1B) or Carlisle Upperby (12B) where it was based at this time before withdrawal from the latter depot during week ending 12th September 1964. *Ray Farrell*

(Right) Stanier Class '5' 4-6-0 No **44675**, a resident at Carlisle Kingmoor (12A) at this time, approaches Preston's Platform 5 with a northbound parcels working on 12th April 1966. The south end of Preston's platforms 5 and 6 were ideal for enthusiasts, given the excellent view afforded of trains approaching from the south. Allocated new to Kingmoor on 18th March 1950, the Class '5' had brief spells at Lostock Hall (24C-10D) and Fleetwood (24F-10C), before returning to the Carlisle Depot during September 1965 and was withdrawn from Kingmoor during week ending 23rd September 1967 to become another victim of the Motherwell Machinery & Scrap Co.Ltd, Wishaw where it was cut-up in February 1968. *Ray Farrell*

PLATFORM 5

Above-centre) Not a train in sight but Preston's Platform 5, looking in a southerly direction, revives memories of a railway that did not just cater for passengers. More or less every train that arrived or departed had some consignment or other to be dealt with by porters, the innumerable trolleys conveniently placed adjacent to the Guards 'Van' or other appropriate vehicle. What would today's Health & Safety criteria be for such mobile platform 'furniture'.

Right) Lostock Hall's Stanier Class '5' 4-6-0 No **44683** the centre of attention as it awaits departure from Platform 5 at Preston with a train for Blackpool on 29th February 1968. Built in July 1950, No 44683 was allocated to Crewe North (5A) when new, before moving to neighbouring South Shed (5B) on 23rd May 1965. After a brief spell at Wigan Springs Branch (8F) the Class '5' moved on to Lostock Hall (24C-10D) on 3th December 1967. Withdrawal came during week ending 13th April 1968 and on 27th August 1968, 44683 was dispatched for cutting up at T.W.Ward, Beighton. *Ray Farrell*

(Above) A Rose Grove (24B-10F) Stanier Class '5' 4-6-0 No **44958** departs Preston's Platform '5' with a train for Blackpool (North) at 14.35 on 4th August 1966. In view of the Motive Power, the train is possibly the 13.53 Blackburn to Blackpool (North), calling all stations prior to Preston and subsequently at Kirkham, Poulton and Layton, but normally scheduled as a DMU working. *Ray Farrell*

(Right) Stanier Class '5' 4-6-0 No **45134** of Carnforth MPD (24L-10A) departs from the north end of Preston Station towards Fishergate Bridge with a Down parcels working on 29th February 1968. The Class '5' was introduced to traffic on 22nd May 1935 at Crewe North (5A) and remained in service until the end of regular BR steam working, being withdrawn from Carnforth on 3rd August 1968. *Ray Farrell*

124

(Above) A southbound freight working, with Stanier Class '5' 4-6-0 No **45293** in charge, runs alongside platform 7, where direct access was gained from the East Lancs (Butler Street) side of Preston Station, on 22nd June 1963. 45293 was introduced to traffic at Shrewsbury (84G) on 23 December 1936. Its last move was to Carlisle Kingmoor (12A) in June 1963, and the locomotive was withdrawn from there during week ending 21 August 1965. *Ray Farrell*

(Centre) A view from the south end of the station looking north along platform 6. The signal box, No 3, an LNWR structure of 1882, controlled a junction with the East Lancashire lines which can just be seen between the end of platform seven and the box. Some five to six years earlier, the station roof had seen some modification which can be noted by comparing with the view above. The canopy to the left would be a forerunner of such facilities up and down the country during the modernisation of the railways of the 1950's. Unfortunately, stations were usually the last to benefit from improvement and it would be many years and privatisation of the industry which enabled adequate resources to be made available.

(Right) Victorian equipment still reigned supreme in the late 1950's when this view south along platform 6 was recorded. The signals here protected the crossovers at mid-point along the platform, the rail layout reflecting patterns of operation which allowed two trains to utilise the one platform, a feature from the &NWR days and quite common practice. The left hand signals controlled access to the East Lancashire Loop line (at the end of the opposite platform). British Railways brave attempts at bringing the station into the 20th century were restricted to platform signing, even the lighting would have to wait its turn.

(Left) Standing alongside the north end of Preston's Platform 5 on 22nd June 1963, the 12.29pm to Workington (Main) awaits departure. The driver of Royal Scot Class '7P' 4-6-0 No **46132**, *The King's Regiment Liverpool*, savours a few thoughtful moments before the departure of his train. In the background the decorative iron parapets of Fishergate Bridge spans the running lines in front of the locomotive with Preston No 4 Signal Box visible beyond. The 'Scot' was a much-travelled locomotive, numbering Polmadie (66A), Camden (1B), Holyhead (6J) and Kentish Town (14B) amongst its bases, before moving to Carlisle Kingmoor (12A) from where it was withdrawn by week ending 1st February 1964.

Ray Farrell

(Below) The south face of Fishergate station approach. The train in the view opposite at

(Right) Just two months before being withdrawn, on Wednesday 1st July 1964, Lostock Hall based Stanier Class 4 2-cylinder 2-6-4T No **42481** takes on water before continuing on its journey to Blackpool Central with the 12.27pm (SX) ex-Liverpool Exchange train which had called at Aintree Sefton Arms and Ormskirk prior to an all-stations run into Preston (arr 1.22pm) via Todd Lane Junction, entering the North Union station from the East Lancashire side. Between 20th June and 5th September, the service ran express to Blackpool Central. Following closure of Central, it was worked into North. It is interesting to see the carriage doors open and the leather straps with which the windows could be raised and lowered, a practice pre-dating the age when door handles became a standard internal fittings.

J W Sutherland

the top of page 127 is alongside platform 8, situated to the far right of the picture below.

Having spent the last 127 pages in the company of trains on our way north to Preston, it is perhaps fitting to leave the railway for a brief nostalgic look at the *Fishergate* of over forty years ago, in September 1963. The cobbled approach (top picture) will forever remain in the minds of passengers familiar with their daily routine of either arriving or leaving the station maybe via a bumpy arrival by taxi. In the centre picture, *County Hall* then, as now, dominates the area of the city whilst a more modest *Austin House* reminds us of the ever growing threat to train travel. At the bottom of the page, *Fishergate* is viewed looking east across the railway bridge with Pitt Street to the left of the picture. I hope you have enjoyed the journey along the 'North Union', thankyou for coming............***Ray Farrell***